REGARDING SUBSTANCE
ABUSE & ADDICTION

REGARDING SUBSTANCE ABUSE & ADDICTION

WHAT YOU NEED TO KNOW. REAL WORLD INSIGHTS FROM FIRSTHAND EXPERIENCE

CRAIG A WILLIAMSON

FLYING WINGS
PUBLISHING

Published by Flying Wings LLC

Front cover by CS Fritz
Editing by E.J. Robison and Kofi Douhadji

ISBN: 979-8-9910565-1-9
Library of Congress Control Number: 2024900736

Printed in the United States of America.

****

FOR CLAY

CONTENTS

ACKNOWLEDGEMENTS

This book acknowledges each one of you on a journey touched by addiction. Those of you personally struggling to get and stay healthy. The legions of loved ones caught up in the fight. The community of treatment professionals, counselors, therapists, those in recovery working the front lines of treatment and medical professionals doing their best in a sea of need.

Despite feeling alone in the shadows, each of you is part of a multitude of fellow travelers dealing with some sort of substance abuse or addiction challenge. This book acknowledges you and your journey.

My family was fortunate to have extraordinary long-term support from a strong, loving treatment professional who I call Dr. M. She was there in thick and thin, communicating in the moments of need regardless of the hour.

To my wife of 35 years, your gift of being both soft and strong makes every moment better. To my daughter Brooke, your inner strength and pure heart shone brightly throughout our family's journey. I am grateful for and proud of you.

You can't walk with someone and pick the path...

PREFACE

In the bewildering journey of addiction, whether you're personally facing challenges or supporting a loved one, uncertainty is around every corner. Each step brings victories, setbacks, joy, and pain. *Regarding Substance Abuse and Addiction* offers practical insights to navigate this complex journey, providing clarity amid confusion. Drawing from my own experiences, this book aims to shed light on the incomprehensible—my way of paying it forward to fellow travelers like you.

This book will reassure you that you're not alone. While every person's experience with this topic is unique, recognizable patterns unite us, offering solace in shared struggles. Substance abuse isn't a chosen path;

we're thrust into its drama by happenstance. None of us intentionally signed up for this ride, yet here we are, seeking understanding and peace.

Ideally, I could be anonymous, but authenticity outweighs anonymity. Readers crave genuine insights from real fellow travelers, not sanitized accounts. By sharing openly, we break the silence surrounding addiction, fostering understanding and support for all on this journey.

Now, I encourage you to utilize the content of this book not as answers, but as a starting point—a spark to light your own torch and support your journey to recovery or to help a loved one on their recovery journey. The information will help you recognize and anticipate circumstances you never would have predicted. Having a "heads up" regarding what might be next can be invaluable as you do your best to find and take next right steps. Let it serve as a guide, a companion, and a source of hope as you navigate the path ahead.

INTRODUCTION

The alerts started to roll in at 4:30 a.m. The sound was familiar and I momentarily ignored it. Amongst other health challenges, my only son Clay battled diabetes. He wore a continuous glucose monitor that transmitted blood sugar readings to his phone as a tool to help manage it. The device pushed alerts to my phone when Clay's sugar levels fell dangerously low.

That morning, the alerts came in nonstop. My wife and I, familiar with the drill, dialed his number repeatedly and tried waking up anyone in his San Diego sober house who might be able to help him. After finally waking a housemate, we learned Clay had ventured to Los Angeles for the weekend—a place previously dreadful and dark for Clay and our family.

His phone eventually went dead, and the agonizing wait began.

As dawn broke, I tried to find solace in a solitary walk along the beach of the San Juan Island we call home. Nature's beauty and the smell of salt water usually offered comfort, but on that day, a foreboding force pressed down on me.

Late that morning, I received a call from our daughter who was sobbing so severely she could not speak coherently. She eventually stammered that Clay had been rushed to an LA hospital in critical condition by a friend who didn't stick around. He passed away at 6:40 a.m. Circumstances were clouded but appeared to include substances.

After a grueling 17-year odyssey, it feels compelling to share some of what I learned. *Regarding Substance Abuse and Addiction* is the book I wish had been there for us, for Clay. It is born from a place of profound loss and a desire to make a positive difference. Your circumstances may not involve a child and are certainly different from mine. However, the basics are likely the same.

You are reading this now for a reason. Perhaps you are in the destructive dance with substance abuse and the little voice in your head is whispering. Or screaming.

Perhaps a loved one is abusing alcohol or another substance and has driven you to wit's end. Perhaps you are being drawn into dysfunction by someone important in your life. You may be working in a treatment or recovery position and feel motivated to better serve. Heaven forbid someone has died, or you have experienced some other painful misfortune related to substance abuse and are trying to make sense of it all. Maybe someone gave you this book hoping you would read it and make better choices.

This book will lay a foundation of practical understanding you can use. It will be valuable for both the individual struggling with substance abuse and those in relationship with substance abusers. It's a journey through the pain and the loss, but also through the learning and wisdom gained (explored more fully in my book *Regarding Things That Matter*). Join me as we explore the shadows of substance abuse and addiction not just to know you are not alone, but to gain knowledge necessary to better care for yourself and others.

It is not possible to speak for the individual challenged by substance use disorder (SUD) without lived experience in those shoes—something I don't have. However, after having been in the storm alongside my son, my hope is you will find this book helpful regardless of the role you play in the drama of substance abuse.

This is not an easy subject to understand, as you likely appreciate already. Some things we know intuitively, and so understanding and insight come easily. Other things can only be learned the hard way— sometimes through excruciating experience. Yet other insights are beyond our comprehension and remain forever a mystery.

Little about SUD is intuitive. Much about it remains a mystery. Intuition has served many of us well and is invaluable on life's journey of challenge and opportunity. But in the case of a first-timer stumbling down the path in a world touched by addiction, intuition comes up short, confused by ignorance and denial.

Let me explain: there were many times in the early years when my "intuition" said we were over the rough patch, which was naive and wrong. With embarrassment, I recall the first time my son was in 30-day inpatient treatment and I helped him lobby to get out two days early because he claimed he was all good. So stupid of me. Hopefully, with the insights shared in this book, you can climb the learning curve quicker, better anticipate the course of events and know how best to respond.

There is no consensus regarding the science, psychology or best strategies to cope with an SUD. It is not necessary, or even helpful, to get stuck on various

SUBSTANCE ABUSE IS COMMON, YET HIDES IN THE BACKGROUND.

nuanced points of view regarding SUD epidemiology (study of distribution, patterns and determinants of disease condition, etc.). Those with real-life experience develop their own understanding as they progress through the school of hard knocks. Substance abuse and addiction do, however, have common patterns, a unique vocabulary, and generally accepted best practices.

Substance abuse is common, yet hides in the background. Things are starting to change, but thus far, substance abuse hasn't become everyday polite conversation. An eye-popping 16.5% of Americans have met the criteria for a substance use disorder, according to The Department of Health and Human Services.[1] Approximately 20% of these individuals suffer from the neurological disease of addiction. We are all eventually touched by someone afflicted with some sort of substance use disorder; having general knowledge will

---

1   https://www.hhs.gov/about/news/2023/01/04/samhsa-announces-national-sur-vey-drug-use-health-results-detailing-mental-illness-substance-use-levels-2021.html

allow you to do better when circumstances inevitably present themselves.

Cultural norms that have historically marginalized addiction are beginning to change. Nearly four percent of the population suffers from the disease of addiction and it seems every family has a story.

This book includes some real-life experiences that have never before been shared. I relate these accounts in the hope they will benefit someone, somewhere, somehow. Hopefully you.

Of most importance now is your story.

REGARDING VOCABULARY

There are many words and expressions used in the substance abuse world that are not part of most people's everyday vocabulary. To keep the discussion clear and helpful, understanding the following basic terms is crucial. As with any complex topic, it is not just about which words you use, but what they truly mean. The following terms are generally accepted and used in this book as defined below.

Addict – person chemically dependent or with the disease of addiction.

Addiction – state of being dependent on something

for daily living. Ensuring or seeking the next "fix" is top priority for an individual with addiction.

Disease of Addiction – medical diagnosis that the American Medical Association (AMA) classified as a disease in 1987.

Chemical Dependency – state of being unable to withdraw substance of abuse without significant consequences; inability to function without substance use.

Clean – the state of being substance-free. Clean time is the amount of time since last substance use, which is referred to as **clean date**.

Cooccurring – condition in which an individual experiences both substance abuse *and* mental disorders. Prolonged substance abuse can lead to mental health disorders that would otherwise not be present.

Denial – the psychological state of not accepting a condition exists contrary to compelling evidence otherwise. Individuals can slip in and out of denial as the brain rationalizes it is okay to use substances. Abusers and their loved ones can experience denial.

Detox – the process often required before acceptance into inpatient treatment. It is a medically supervised lockdown or blackout period in which the abuser's system adjusts to being substance-free (referred to as **withdrawal**). Three to five days is a typical detox period. In the case of alcohol, detox can be life-threatening.

Drug of Choice – the preferred substance of a substance abuser. Alcohol is the most common, fentanyl is among the most deadly.

Enablement – protecting the substance abuser from the full consequences of their behavior.

Inpatient Treatment – treatment in a structured living environment with limited contact with the outside world. Structure typically includes scheduled programming of meals, group therapy, individual therapy, visitation and lights-out hours. Inpatient treatment can last anywhere from 30 days to nine months.

11

Intake – process associated with entering detox or inpatient treatment. Often an emotionally charged time as patients vacillate about willingness to enter treatment.

Intensive Outpatient (IOP) – treatment phase after inpatient. Patients can live outside of treatment but are required to attend daily morning and afternoon treatment sessions along with 12-step meetings several days a week.

Involuntary Hold – legal process in which an individual deemed to be a threat to themselves or others can be held against their will. Hold period is typically 72 hours at a public psychiatric facility with a separate adjudication process to extend the hold period if necessary. Each state has its own specific rules regarding involuntary holds.

Loved One – family member, friend or anyone in the mix and concerned about the welfare of the afflicted person.

MAOI's – class of psychiatric medications that are psychoactive in a manner that makes them unsuitable for people with the disease of addiction.

Recovery – ongoing process of staying substance-free. Since substance use disorder and disease of addiction are "incurable" and risk of relapse never goes away, recovery is a lifelong process.

Rock Bottom – an experience substance abusers have in their darkest moments, oftentimes capitulating to treatment, religious conversion or committing to recovery whatever it takes.

Sober House – group living environment in which residents pledge to remain sober and comply with house rules. Regular drug testing is typically required. Enforcement of house rules runs the gambit from very strict to very casual.

Sobriety – substance-free.

Sponsor – a more experienced substance abuser who is succeeding in recovery and has agreed to be a support resource for someone not as far along in their recovery.

Substance – any mind-altering substance. Alcohol, opioids, cocaine, methamphetamine, barbiturates, and THC are typical examples.

Substance Abuse – broad term used to describe continued use of mind-altering substances despite negative consequences.

SUD – substance use disorder. This condition involves the excessive use of substances, including alcohol and drugs, leading to significant impairment or distress. SUD is characterized by an inability to control substance use, putting a higher priority on substance use than other obligations and continuing to use substances despite the harm it causes.

Tough Love – approach used by people in relationship with substance abusers. The idea is to withhold support or interaction of any kind unless the substance abuser is successful in recovery.

UA – urine analysis drug test.

Now that we are on the same page with these key terms, let's get started.

REGARDING SUBSTANCE USE DISORDER (SUD) VS. DISEASE OF ADDICTION

Substance use disorder (SUD) is a term that captures a range of behaviors, varying from life-threatening substance abuse to challenging periods in someone's life. Imagine a continuum: at one end, disease of addiction represents a profound brain chemistry anomaly, making exposure to any mind-altering substance uncontrollable. This condition, without intervention, can be fatal. Treatment demands complete abstinence and significant lifestyle changes to maintain sobriety, a journey fraught with difficulty and extensively discussed in this book.

Elsewhere on this spectrum, substance misuse often arises from the pursuit of pleasure, escape from pain or as a method to cope with life's challenges—not necessarily from the same biochemical imbalance seen with the disease of addiction. Self-medication to dull emotional pain or escape problems is common, but it doesn't stem from the same root as disease of addiction.

Understanding the distinction between general substance misuse and disease of addiction is crucial. It's like coming to a fork in the road: though both paths may lead to darkness, they're driven by different forces. Recognizing your path can better your chances of progress, though tragically, distinguishing between disease and controllable behavior is often challenging, sometimes requiring a cycle of relapse and profound honesty.

For those with addiction, the brain's malfunction leaves them unable to moderate their use of any substance. Total abstinence is essential for recovery.

Substance abusers who do not have the disease of addiction can restore health by learning why they abuse substances and addressing the root causes and mentality. Many people carry unresolved pain from their origin stories or life experiences and use substances to escape or seek relief. With counseling and maturity, it is possible to move beyond the pain and remove the need to escape. Over time, they can replace abusing substances with other more positive coping or pleasure-seeking behaviors. Total lifelong abstinence may not be essential for these people. Of course, the gold standard for recovery is total abstinence from all substances, and suggesting anything less is sacrilegious to a person with the disease of addiction.

In my youth, especially in college with all the new-found freedom it brought, it seemed like everyone loved to party, which invariably involved substances. It seemed like most of us minored in partying. Beer and marijuana were staple foods and no one seemed to think much of it. Most of us got our young rebellious yahoos out and moved on to professional lives and reasonably healthy routines.

I had one friend, however, who went in a different direction. Cocaine became part of his persona and lifestyle. While it was fun to be together at first, his cocaine usage eventually crowded everything else out, including our friendship. He was clearly on a dangerous, intensifying path and our interactions became less frequent, shorter and more superficial. He couldn't stay focused long enough to talk. I, along with other observers, worried things would not end well and didn't know what to do. It seemed like no voice was loud enough to break through the screams in his head to keep partying.

Then it got worse, to the point of a three-day

hospitalization for medical stabilization. My friend got scared, but not of what you might think. It wasn't the prospect of death that scared him most; it was the fear of being a loser in the world. He came from down low, if you know what I mean. He didn't want others to think he was a lost cause. His self-esteem and aspirations for a better life were strong enough to steer a change. He turned his ship back to sanity and built an amazing life. Substance abuse never again risked foreclosing his future. He did not have the disease of addiction and is able to consume responsibly—for the most part.

You may be familiar with the notion of a "functioning" alcoholic, which is a very real thing. Within the midrange of the SUD continuum, there is an army of substance abusers who "function" on an ongoing basis. They live a daily routine that involves substance use followed by a rally to show up, get by and then repeat.

THERE IS NO BLOOD TEST OR SOME OTHER SORT OF PHYSICAL MARKER INDICATING THE DISEASE OF ADDICTION IS PRESENT.

Oftentimes, the substance use takes place in relative secrecy, at least for a while.

I was amazed by an employee early in my career who was a functioning alcoholic. He was able to drink to a stupor

18

late in the day only to arise early and make a showing at work the next day. The physical capacity required to live this way was remarkable. As you might expect, it was also not sustainable. There were days when he was missing in action without explanation, leading to his eventual firing—which was hard to do considering he was a good, capable guy at the core. Not surprisingly, his profile included frequent job changes and a trail of broken relationships. His story is all too common.

DISEASE OF ADDICTION

The American Medical Association classified the disease of addiction in 1987. Unfortunately, unlike with many diseases, there is no blood test or some other sort of physical marker indicating the disease of addiction is present. The condition does tend to run in family lines with hereditary patterns. Diagnostic criteria for the disease of addiction are six or more of the following:

1. Using more of a substance than intended or using it for longer than you're meant to.
2. Trying to cut down or stop using the substance but being unable to.
3. Experiencing intense cravings or urges to use the substance.

4. Needing more of the substance to get the desired effect—also called tolerance.
5. Developing withdrawal symptoms when not using the substance.
6. Spending more time getting and using drugs and recovering from substance use.
7. Neglecting responsibilities at home, work or school because of substance use.
8. Continuing to use, even when it causes relationship problems.
9. Giving up important or desirable activities due to substance use.
10. Using substances in risky settings that put you in danger.
11. Continuing to use despite damage to your physical and mental health.

The human brain is a physical thing with physical properties, including a dynamic, complex chemistry. This chemistry is carefully balanced to regulate pleasure, judgment, and survival instincts. When stimulated, such as by mind-altering substances, receptor cells in the brain release dopamine, inducing feelings of pleasure. For a healthy brain, this experience is temporary, with the judgment center and survival instinct ensuring a return to equilibrium once the substance wears off.

However, in the case of a diseased brain, the story unfolds quite differently. Here, the stimulation of receptor cells triggers uncontrollable multiplication akin to a chia pet gone wild. These rogue cells effectively hijack the brain, overpowering the judgment center and survival instinct. This phenomenon marks the onset of addiction, rendering the individual powerless to resist continued substance use. The cycle perpetuates, with cravings intensifying and substance use escalating.

At first, pleasure may have been the driving force behind substance use, but as addiction takes hold, the motivation shifts. The individual no longer seeks to feel good but rather to avoid feeling bad, trapped in a desperate bid to stave off withdrawal symptoms. An individual suffering and in need of a "fix" is commonly referred to as "sick." Despite insinuations otherwise, the individual in active addiction is not having fun. They are trapped in a twisted dance with pain and, many times, untimely death. Understanding this truth should evoke compassion and empathy for individuals battling addiction.

> ULTIMATELY, ADDICTION IS GIVING UP EVERYTHING FOR ONE THING.

Ultimately, addiction is giving up everything for one thing.

Success in recovery is possible but outrageously difficult. Tragically, once clean and in recovery, a one-time slip has the perfect relapse hook. Nothing horrible happens. Last night's "one time" use was deserved because of fill in the blank (promotion at work, anniversary date of being sober, etc.). And look—I'm just fine today. I can handle it, obviously. So, no problem with just a little tonight. Before you know it—BOOM! The cycle is reactivated. Powerless yet again.

Disease of addiction is not correlated with IQ, social status, education, character, discipline, upbringing, support systems, religiosity, etc. It does have hereditary tendencies and frequently runs in family lines. There also appears to be some correlation with race as it relates to certain indigenous groups such as Native Americans.

Disease of addiction, and for that matter substance abuse in general, is accompanied by some rotten realities. Deception, for example. Lying, deceit and manipulation are acquired skills the addiction monster spawns to keep feeding itself—even if the affected person is inherently honest and of good character. The resultant wreckage of relationships, careers, finances and health is profoundly sad. And entirely predictable.

Similar brain chemistry associated with substance-related addiction can be found in other forms of apparent addiction—pornography, gaming and gambling, for example.

Alcoholism remains a confusing term. Given alcohol's acceptance and availability, it is the most common substance of abuse. Many people who do not have the disease of addiction drink to excess and can cut back and be reasonably healthy. For others, the problem is more serious and the addiction model of total abstinence is the only real solution. The confusing part is the way society tends to focus on alcohol and not the underlying SUD. I would encourage you to understand alcoholism to be like any other SUD we are seeking to understand in this book. Keep in mind that an individual with SUD will generally abuse a different substance if their "drug of choice" is not an option. Removing the alcohol from an alcoholic may not resolve the underlying SUD.

Chemical dependency is a real thing. Unfortunately, it is not a reliable indicator of the disease of addiction. Someone abusing substances as a coping mechanism can become physically dependent without necessarily having the organic disease of addiction.

Drug of choice is another confusing notion. Mistakenly, many people think that removing the drug of choice—alcohol or opioids for example—will fix the problem. Not for the person with the disease of addiction. Denied one mind-altering substance, they will seek another. The only effective treatment is total abstinence from all mind-altering substances.

REGARDING PROGRESSION
AND PHASES

Addiction progresses in phases. To say the process is nonlinear is an understatement; it's akin to a full-on rodeo. There is no set of time for each phase and individuals often find themselves moving back and forth between them.

1. **Denial.** Denial is the starting point for both the user and their loved ones. It is common to oscillate in and out of denial. Some individuals remain in this phase indefinitely, even as they progress through the stages below.

2. **Secret use.** Being around a user during this cat-and-mouse phase is confusing and frus-

trating for loved ones. It can be all-consuming for the user as they are preoccupied with acquiring and secretly using.

3. **Defiant use.** As the substance abuse problem becomes known to both the user and loved ones, defiance sets in. The user insists it is their business alone, they can handle it and use in defiance of pleas not to.

4. **Open use.** At this stage, nothing else matters to the user except using. They no longer have the energy or patience to hide their habit and may use openly in front of loved ones.

5. **Premature death.** Left untreated, or unsuccessfully treated, addiction inevitably leads to premature death.

Individuals with the disease of addiction are rendered powerless over substances and often find themselves trapped in an escalating pattern of use, progressing from one substance to another. For example, my son progressed through an array of substances, starting with alcohol all the way up (down, actually) to injecting meth. The pattern for an addict will continue until stopped by outside forces like imprisonment, hospitalization or an involuntary hold order. Some sort of hitting bottom is required that physically prevents continued use. Submitting to inpatient treatment is usually the best option.

Substance abusers without the disease of addiction are not entirely powerless against substances. They can make a conscious decision to change course and take steps back toward sobriety before their SUD progresses to a point of no return.

Navigating SUD presents vexing challenges. Unlike healing from a broken bone, the process is not linear but rather nonlinear and individualized. Understanding the root of the problem can be elusive and frustrating, as it involves a complex interplay of factors such as pleasure-seeking, pain-numbing, coping mechanisms, environmental influences, social pressures and psychological dynamics. Yet, it's essential to undertake the humbling work of honestly uncovering the reasons behind substance abuse to halt the progression toward premature death.

REGARDING DENIAL

Denial is the insidious host of substance abuse, lurking in the background and affecting both the user and their loved ones. In an effort to maintain harmony, loved ones often subconsciously gravitate toward denial, while users cling to it as a means to perpetuate their substance abuse. For users, denial is part of SUD.

Denial can take many forms and exist in psychological layers. Circumstances can provide a venue for denial when clues and facts indicating something is wrong are dismissed or minimized. As a defense

DENIAL IS THE INSIDIOUS HOST OF SUBSTANCE ABUSE.

mechanism, or perhaps to avoid conflict, we fail to acknowledge unreasonable behavior. For example, our loved one didn't come home until morning, or they were totally out of it yesterday...but that happens to everyone sometimes. Denial reasons there is no point in making a big deal out of it or pushing for an explanation. Things are fine.

Denial of the underlying substance use disorder can be a defense mechanism, trying to protect one from fear and pain. Denial mentality can include thoughts such as the following: "It's just a phase," "Things will get better," "The substance abuser promised to clean up their act," or "Life is already hard enough for everyone involved and there is no point in escalating things by calling out the problem." Denial provides shelter from bad news and an even darker reality.

Another form of denial involves the substance abuser comparing themselves to someone worse off. "Look at John, he lost his job and family; I'll never get so bad I lose my family"—until the person does lose his family and then picks a lower point of comparison. "Look at Dave, he declared bankruptcy and spent time in jail. I'll never lose all my money"—until it happens and an even lower comparison is set, keeping denial alive.

Denial can try to split hairs or distort reality. Remembering that SUD exists on a continuum, some afflicted individuals will acknowledge they have a challenge but argue "it isn't that bad." They say things like "I can quit when I want." The broken logic suggests "being honest" about having an issue somehow forgives denying the severity of the problem.

DENIAL CAN COME AND GO BUT NEVER STOPS TRYING TO TAKE OVER.

Denial spreads its influence to more than just the actual substance abuse. Oftentimes, the consequences of SUD behavior are also ignored. Legal, medical, career and relationship issues can be denied or trivialized. It is not uncommon for deadlines (paying a fine, for example) or important appointments such as court dates to be missed while the individual with an SUD denies their importance and believes (hopes) they will just go away.

Denial is extremely difficult to overcome. In some ways, it is like naturally curly hair; you can work hard to straighten it out, but the curls return before you know it. Denial can come and go but never stops trying to take over.

Denial is a serious threat even to people well along

in recovery. A period of success in recovery can actually open the door to denial as the individual with an SUD comes to believe their success proves they don't have a problem. The addict's brain is constantly trying to convince itself it's okay to use just this one time. A couple of beers never hurt anyone... The door of denial just needs to open a crack and the devil of relapse slips in.

REGARDING BEHAVIOR

There are all sorts of challenging behaviors substance abusers display. Since each person and circumstance is different, it is not possible to predict or know what you will experience. Some of the behaviors are obvious to any observer. Others are hidden or harder to detect unless you have close, consistent contact with the user. Some behaviors are persistent and repetitive. There may be behaviors other people experience that never show up in your situation.

Behaviors can vary depending on the specific substance being abused and

BEHAVIORS CAN VARY DEPENDING ON THE SPECIFIC SUBSTANCE BEING ABUSED.

how far the individual has progressed into the abuse cycle. For example, methamphetamines are uppers and can lead to impulsiveness, risky behavior and hyperactivity. Opioid abuse can result in confusion and depression.

The sampling below is provided to help prepare you and give reassurance you are not alone. Don't be surprised if the substance abuser denies or responds defensively if the behaviors are pointed out.

MANIPULATION BECOMES A CORE COMPETENCY FOR USERS.

- **Minimization**. Users minimize the severity of things that happen, bad decisions, usage and impact on others, often resorting to outright dishonesty to justify their substance use.
- **Disappearing act**. Users inexplicably vanish, ignoring calls and messages, only to reappear later as if nothing happened, dismissing any concerns raised.
- **Manipulation**. Manipulation becomes a core competency for users. They employ creative tactics to facilitate their substance use, often enlisting unwitting accomplices along the way.
- **Dishonesty**. Users resort to bending the truth and outright lying to keep using. Like manipu-

lation, they become quite skilled at dishonesty. Paradoxically, this is true even for the inherently honest person. Thinking is distorted by the SUD, resulting in behavior that frequently does not reflect a true self.

- **Isolation.** Users distance themselves from loved ones, seeking privacy and avoiding confrontation, often closing themselves off from meaningful relationships. Even when living under the same roof as their loved ones, closed doors become physical barriers and the demand for privacy becomes non-negotiable.
- **Mood swings.** Users experience rapid and intense mood swings, reflecting the tumultuous nature of addiction.
- **Repetition/Fixation.** Substance abusers often fixate on certain ideas or behaviors, repeating them compulsively as part of their addictive cycle.
- **Sleep disruption** is a red flag as the SUD escalates. This means sometimes sleeping all day, or even for days on end, which overlaps with the isolation tendency above. It can go the other way with the individual being up all night, sometimes for days on end. The inability to sleep is an onset indicator of a dangerous

manic cycle that can result from extended use
of some substances. Attempts by loved ones
to address the concern are met with denial,
minimization and more isolation.

- **Time distortion.** For example, insisting
something is "taking forever" and they can't wait
or "it was just an hour" when half a day passed.
There can be confusion between night and day
deeper into substance abuse cycles.

- **Relationship issues** of all types. According to
the user, these are invariably the other person's
fault. Broken families, marriages and relationships litter the path of substance abusers. The
dysfunction is stressful for everyone involved
and tends to drive the substance abuser deeper
into substance abuse in an effort to cope and
run from the pain of it all.

This sort of obvious negative feedback loop
can fuel failure spirals as things get worse and
worse. Loops like this show up in many different ways besides relationships such as the stress
of financial reversal, poor self-care in areas
such as diet and exercise, disruption in living
arrangements, financial issues, etc.

- **Job loss** is common. The individual often insists it is because the employer was unreasonable and/or it was someone else's fault.
- **Money issues** are common as poor choices and their related costs pile up. Many times things such as late rent, unpaid fines or medical bills result in penalties that only multiply financial burden. "Loaning" a substance abuser money in an effort to help is tempting but almost never productive (see Enablement chapter).
- **Defensiveness.** Users react defensively to any suggestion of wrongdoing, dismissing concerns and deflecting blame.
- **Neglect of personal care.** Users can neglect personal hygiene and appearance, exhibiting erratic behavior and deteriorating physical health.
- **Theft.** At first, it might be something borrowed that somehow never got returned. Later, it can be outright stealing from loved ones and strangers. Once again, this behavior is really not related to a person's underlying character or propensity to steal. Even the most honest of individuals will do what is required to keep using once powerless to their SUD.

- **Impulsivity**. Individuals with an SUD can do crazy, dangerous things on a whim. Impulsiveness sometimes results from the need to get more substance. Addicts spend a lot of time and energy maintaining a supply. Typically, buys are small, which necessitates finding more again soon. Resupply is in small quantities because it is less dangerous if caught and less expensive to obtain with money being tight. Subconsciously, the user may know they need to stop using and believe this next time will be the last before they "quit," so no need to acquire more substance than needed that moment.

- **Rage or hysteria**. This is a hard one to endure. As the user's mind and body get more stressed with the negative consequences of using, they can sometimes snap. Stay calm and don't add energy. Let it blow itself out. It usually doesn't take long, even if it feels like forever.

- **Fabricated stories,** sometimes unbelievable on the face, become part of interacting with users. They attempt to explain odd things that happen with stories you want to believe. Over time, you learn to recognize these as just another story. One common aspect of most stories is they deflect responsibility for negative or unintended consequences to others.

- **Higher Power Encounters.** Deep into the grip of substance abuse, it is not unusual for the user to begin referencing God in ways they previously did not. They can insist God has taken an active role in directing their thoughts and actions. At first, the references to God may bring loved ones comfort, wanting to believe something redemptive may be happening. Don't get your hopes up. Almost certainly there is a more sinister dynamic unfolding that involves cognitive distortion resulting from substance abuse or perhaps another flavor of manipulation since no one wants to argue with someone embracing the Lord.

- **Excessive use of substitutes.** Smoking, vaping and caffeine consumption become compulsive behaviors, providing temporary relief from cravings.

- **False victory proclamations.** Users may declare false breakthroughs or commitments to recovery, only to revert to old habits shortly afterward, perpetuating the cycle of addiction.

Addiction-related behaviors are not limited to substance abuse. Gambling involves the same brain chemistry phenomenon of pleasure-producing dopamine overpowering judgment. For example, my son Clay was exceptionally intelligent and fell into options trading on the Robinhood platform. There were periods he literally could not stop. Despite the obvious irrationality of it all, the platform (and others) continued to allow trading and even borrowing to do so. Occasional account lockouts due to negative balances created emergencies for Clay as his brain demanded the continued dopamine stimulation that came from gambling. He would open accounts on other apps and sadly turn back to substances under the grip of addiction. We are beginning to see acknowledgment that this same sort of brain phenomenon is being exploited in the digital domain with social media and even pornography.

Some people use the expression "having an addictive personality" to describe this pattern of addiction. I do not like this expression because it implies a psychological trait or mentality is the driver rather than an actual chemical malfunction taking place in the brain of an addict.

REGARDING EPISODES

Episodes involve extreme circumstances and are very difficult to experience. They are always shocking and can be unimaginable brushes with crisis and even death. These episodes result from the irrational, erratic behavior of the substance abuser, or even sometimes others reacting to provocative behavior on the part of the substance abuser. Accidents, fighting, disturbances of all kinds, interactions with law enforcement and medical emergencies are typical scenarios.

Episodes are inevitable for the severe substance abuser. Sometimes, there is a buildup of tension or conflict, making it obvious something is going to go wrong. Sometimes, a crisis seems to burst onto the scene suddenly, eclipsing everything else for everyone else. Trying to avoid incidents is certainly a good idea and sometimes the risk blows over, but sometimes this isn't the case and you have no choice but to ride it out.

When the substance abuser is struggling with stability, the risk of an episode increases later in the day. The expression "sundowning" refers to this phenomenon.

Episodes can be both public and private. My family has experienced public episodes involving helicopter rescues, countless ambulance transports (many of which I'll never know about), hospital emergency rooms, auto accidents, arrests, police stations, jails and homeless encampments. Oddly enough, an episode happening in public can be a good thing. Other people often join the fray to help.

My son had a complex medical profile that included diabetes, Addison's Disease and the disease of addiction. He was medically brittle and constantly at risk of death resulting from the interaction of his conditions. As a result, many of our episodes involved medical complexity and risks. I became highly skilled at providing rapid-fire medical briefings to first responders and emergency room doctors and nurses.

Private episodes take place at home and can be frightening. Most of us never imagine calling 9-1-1, especially to our home, but I ended up becoming very familiar with how things work. Don't be afraid to make the call, but consider it a last resort. If more than one loved one is present, keep each other calm, work as a team and make the decision together. First responders are usually very good but are not miracle workers.

Once first responders are on-site, the next decision becomes whether to transport the individual to a hospital or not. Being admitted to a hospital can be a very positive step toward improvement or even recovery. Some people report being taken by ambulance and hospitalized as a life-transforming experience (see the Hitting Bottom chapter).

Loved ones may not be able to fix or avoid an episode, but they can do a lot to avoid unnecessarily escalating the situation. Stay calm, do not lose composure or start yelling. Identify other people in the immediate mix and work together.

The episodes in my life took place with a 15-29 year old medically brittle child, which greatly affected my role and experience. Different situations will certainly have their own unique challenges. For example, your child being in an unknown location, which was often the case for me, multiplies uncertainty and urgency. In the case of a married couple, where one partner is struggling with SUD, being apart and temporarily out of contact may be a relief.

Often, the incident takes place away from you and the cell phone is your primary tool. Scrambling to reach out is necessary to connect with others actually present or in recent contact with the user. It helps to have teammates who keep as much information flowing as possible. Text is most efficient by far. Pay special attention to who is in which group texts; you have a different vibe depending on who is in the group. Sometimes you can get a thread going with friends of the substance abuser and you want to connect with them in a way that will keep the thread alive.

Share information with teammates to get a better understanding of what is happening and why. Action is thickest when authorities are present. I always felt an urgency to pass along medical conditions and meds requirements info. In emergency room situations it usually took a few tries and involved informing nurses first. I got to speak many times to actual attending physicians. Respecting their time, I tried hard to deliver a concise, rapid-fire briefing, which more than once helped save Clay's life.

An episode may or may not be a "hitting bottom" event. Although counterintuitive, there is merit to hoping the incident is severe enough to scare the user into treatment and onto a path of recovery. These challenging moments provide a chance for loved ones to help guide the user into treatment.

REGARDING LOVING A
SUBSTANCE ABUSER

You can't walk with someone and pick the path. Loving a substance abuser can be unbelievably challenging. It can feel like a rollercoaster of hope, fear, frustration and bewilderment. At times, all you want is to get off but there is no way to stop the night-mare. In fact, the ride tends to get more and more intense, and you never know when the

> YOU CAN'T WALK WITH SOMEONE AND PICK THE PATH.

next gut-wrenching curve will hit. It is even more vexing when the substance abuser is a minor, whether living at home or not. Parents, guardians and family feel a heightened responsibility to assist and protect.

47

In the beginning, rabbit holes of good intentions are hard to avoid. It takes time to learn the ropes of a life touched by substance abuse. For example, when first learning of a loved one's substance abuse, a common question, especially if a minor or illicit substance is involved, is "Where did they get the substance!?" There is an understandable impulse to track down the source and hold them accountable somehow. If only it could be that easy. The truth is any substance is available anytime to someone who wants it. There is an ever-present supply network invisible to outsiders. This has always been the case, but the invisible supply network is even more efficient in today's digital communication world.

ANY SUBSTANCE IS AVAILABLE ANYTIME TO SOMEONE WHO WANTS IT.

Other rabbit holes include things like trying to prohibit contact with bad influences or restricting places the abuser can go. Well-intended onlookers are usually quick to ask "Who are they hanging around with?" This is a reasonable question, but a dead end nonetheless. Yes, the cast of characters may be a bad influence. No, you don't make things better by villainizing third parties. It only makes you less safe to confide in or communicate with.

Another unhelpful rabbit hole of sorts is being concerned about what other people think. It is normal to fear you will somehow be defined by experiencing SUD or being in a relationship with someone struggling with an SUD. We all want to be accepted, so the concern is understandable, but not helpful. Do your best to get over concerns about what others think. True friends will be just that. Others will come and go. So be it.

Yet another type of rabbit hole is getting stuck on proclaiming the irrational, self-destructive implications of substance abuse behavior. By all means, point out the folly and risk of it all. After all, speaking truth is part of being authentic and it might actually make an impression on the substance abuser. Having said that, substance abuse is by nature irrational and destructive. Shouting it incessantly from your mountaintop of sobriety will not be helpful and is not the hill to die on. You are right. So now what?

Many of us are problem solvers and want to get things done, but SUD is not a problem that can be solved by well-intended observers. One life wisdom suggests that "control is an illusion," which is certainly the case with SUD. The same is true when it comes to time. Each person's journey through an SUD unfolds in its own due time. As much as loved ones might want to rush the clock, they can't. Imposing time limits for various milestones is unrealistic and generally not helpful. Things typically take longer to play out than desired. Set your expectations accordingly to avoid experiencing more anxiety than there already is.

Remember that things are not always as they appear. For example, we live on an island on a waterfront property. I recall sitting on the deck as a huge eagle plunged into the glassy bay to snag an unsuspecting salmon. It was a sight to behold as the eagle began flight with the salmon in tow. However, when the fish's tail didn't rise fully out of the water, I realized the fish was too heavy for the eagle to get airborne. After a couple more tries, the eagle's performance got worse, resulting in its struggling in the water. The would-be predator was eventually forced to take a much-needed break. After resting, the great bird began a preposterous swimming motion with its wings, eventually reaching shore with fish in tow. Soon, a feeding frenzy began. I couldn't believe my eyes—nor how tenacious the eagle was.

A few years passed, and I shared the story with a local. Remarkably, he had a similar story, but it ended differently. Apparently, if an eagle grabs a fish too big to handle, it is unable to withdraw its talons for retreat. If the fish is too big, it can eventually pull the eagle under-

water, never to resurface again. That is what my acquain-
tance witnessed.

I share this firsthand story to make a point. I saw
with my own eyes and "knew" exactly what happened.
Only, I was completely wrong. The eagle was in grave
danger, not dominating as I initially thought during
my encounter. Things are
not always as they appear in
the orbit of someone with
an SUD. Don't be naive, and
don't be paranoid; try to find
a healthy place in the middle.

RELATIONSHIPS ARE
THE GLUE OF HOPE.

As a loved one, you lose sleep. You get flaky with
your schedule: arriving late, leaving early or not showing
up as you deal with weird things that keep happening.
You spend money you can't afford trying to fix problems
you can't fix. You miss meals due to lack of appetite—or
binge eat without realizing it. At times you don't feel
comfortable in your own home and your heart races
when the phone rings or there is a knock at the door.

Sometimes, things are calm and you feel better,
only to be thrust back into crisis by what happens next.
It can be a hard life.

Relationships are the glue of hope. Communication is the lifeblood of relationships but can shut down
with the strain of substance abuse. This brings us to a

very important insight. Although it may be difficult, there is wisdom in doing whatever it takes to keep the door of communication open. Loved ones ghosting loved ones serves no one. A way to improve the odds of keeping communication alive is to differentiate between the individual as a person and their negative behavior. You can reject and condemn specific behavior without rejecting the person. For example, you can make your disdain for being drunk known while allowing the abuser to feel your love and support for positive progress. There may come a time when the substance abuser's most valuable resource, and perhaps turning point for good, is their relationship with you. Keep it alive through thick and thin.

Having said that, keeping the relationship alive is often not possible or right—especially in the case of marriage relationships. In the case of a couple where one is battling with the disease of addiction, there comes a point when a spouse cannot and/or should not continue to put up with the pain and dysfunction associated with substance abuse. The threshold for "leaving" varies by individual, of course, but everyone has a breaking point. The discord leading up to separation takes a huge toll on everyone involved, and then the actual physical separation is gut-wrenching. Usually, all the stress tragically serves to drive the substance abuser deeper into addiction.

Transportation can often pose challenges for loved ones supporting someone with an SUD. From issues like loss of driver's license to car damage or the financial strain of rideshare services, transportation hurdles can become significant burdens. These challenges not only affect daily logistics but can also impede essential tasks like attending court dates or securing better job opportunities.

In the midst of these difficulties, loved ones play a crucial role in providing support. Whether it's offering rides, helping with car repairs, or exploring alternative transportation options, their assistance can alleviate some of the stress and obstacles faced by individuals dealing with SUD. By actively addressing transportation needs, loved ones can contribute to creating a more stable environment conducive to recovery and progress.

The impact on families reverberates for generations. Yes, there are the sadly damaged or broken relationships. There are also the damaged individuals. Children can spend a lifetime coming to terms with how they were affected by a substance-abusing parent. Feelings of rejection, anger and fear take a long time to resolve. Oddly enough, guilt can be an issue as children tend to subconsciously think family trauma is somehow their fault. If this is you, take heart. I have a close friend from a home traumatized and broken by alcohol who eventually was able to throw off the unhealthy feelings and thinking stemming from his childhood experience. He is now a rockstar physician and a positive beacon of light for countless others.

Loved ones will benefit from staying close to each other. Take turns being the strong one, the calm one, the talker or the listener. Support each other with love and acceptance even when you have different ideas about what to do next. Working challenges together can bring you closer, one of those blessings in disguise.

SUD and addiction result in horribly selfish behavior. By definition, a substance abuser is preoccupied with meeting their own relentless need. The needs of others are crowded out, leaving loved ones depleted from giving without receiving much in return. This is not personal. It is just the way it is. Don't become disabled and wounded in the trap of hurt feelings or unmet expectations. Doing so serves no one.

When things go wrong, it is not helpful to feel guilty about your role in any way. You already have enough emotion to cope with; do not allow regret to be in the mix. It is not your fault. You didn't cause the underlying problem. You can't fix it. For sure, learn as you go and let this learning be reflected as the situations progress, but do not fall into the trap of thinking maybe you could have done better. You are doing the very best you can. Everyone is.

There is no way out of experiencing pain and bewilderment when loving someone with an SUD. For me, a dark moment of bewilderment came when trying to see any path to my son's survival. I remember journaling "No sightline to light...all directions dark." I just couldn't see any way out. Then it got better—for a while. (More on this later.)

The burdens of guilt and shame carried by substance abusers are real. Maintaining healthy self-esteem understandably becomes very difficult. These burdens complicate the quest for sobriety because using substances is already ingrained as a way to mask negative feelings. The more one uses, the more guilty they feel. The more guilt they feel, the more they use. This sort of vicious negative feedback cycle is inherent in the SUD world and shows up in all sorts of ways.

Some substance abusers overcompensate by being brash or appearing overconfident. Others retreat, disconnect and isolate. Many cycle back and forth between both postures. Well-intended loved ones piling on to shame a person, especially someone with the disease of addiction, is not helpful. When it comes to rejection, it is important to differentiate between rejecting behavior as opposed to the person.

REGARDING SELF-CARE

Ultimately, loved ones must realize they need to take care of themselves **first**. Being stressed out, losing sleep, canceling activities you enjoy, not eating right, losing your temper, etc. compromises your ability to be a force for good. It's only a matter of time before this insight suddenly hits: you can't be part of the answer if you become part of the problem.

How are **you** doing now if you're under the load of loving someone in active addiction? Don't let yourself become sick while carrying the burden.

"LOVE WITH DETACHMENT" IS THE GOLD STANDARD FOR LOVED ONES.

"Love with detachment" is the gold standard for loved ones. This enlightened mentality provides a foundation to take care of yourself first.

Finding someone to talk to is part of self-care. Not everyone wants to, or should, hear the sometimes gory details of your journey. At the same time, hiding your situation from others is probably not a good idea, given the importance of living authentically. Not everyone is a suitable confidant, though. Work to find the right person/people you can lean on and then lean in. Sometimes, your normal go-to person lacks the listening skills or maturity to be a good fit. No worries, you will find people to share with. Some will find you.

Being listened to helps you feel better when sharing with the right person. Good listeners have the ability to support you without suggesting solutions. Professional counseling, while expensive (sometimes covered by insurance), is valuable for many. Treatment programs typically have programming for loved ones and can provide a safe temporary support community. For me, informally verbalizing to friends or family is a way of testing thoughts and feelings. Sometimes, I hear myself say something and don't agree with the notion after hearing it out loud. Conversation is a way to clarify thinking and deepen relationships.

There are resources for loved ones of substance abusers—Alcoholics Anonymous (Al-Anon) groups, for example. My dear friend Jeff found comfort and insight in the bag of shit exercise at an Al-Anon meeting. The exercise is powerful and goes like this: Everyone in attendance takes turns sharing their personal bag of shit story associated with loving a substance abuser. The stories are horrific and tears flood the room. Each person puts their figurative bag in the middle when done talking. At the end, each person gets to take any bag they want for their own. Despite being certain at the start no one could possibly have it worse, every participant ends up taking back their own bag. Maybe their situation is not the worst imaginable after all. You come to understand that it could always be worse.

Al-Anon-type groups are an invaluable source of connection and knowledge. Yes, you benefit from the fellowship and support. Don't forget, however, that your words, spirit and energy can be a blessing to others— which in itself can be very satisfying. Sometimes just being a heartbeat in the mix is helpful to others. All the brokenness out there provides us a chance to model grace under the gun.

It is paramount to keep yourself sane and healthy amid the chaos of having a loved one dealing with the disease of addiction. Challenging moments are to be expected and it is crucial to have healthy disciplines in place to keep from becoming a mess yourself. What are your coping mechanisms?

The following are a few factors that provide a window into how well you are coping:

- Remember Maslow's Hierarchy of Needs? It is depicted as a triangle enclosing layers one on top of the other. The idea is that layers on top can only be supported by strong layers below. Life is the same. Diet, hydration, exercise and rest are the foundation. Without these pillars, it is hard to function optimally in a dynamic world. Start with the basics of healthy eating, regular exercise and plenty of sleep in caring for yourself.
- Your own enabling behavior is recognized and under control. Finding the right posture regarding enabling takes time, and circumstances vary. The idea here is that you are self-aware, rational and deliberate when it comes to when and how you assist someone struggling with an SUD.
- You maintain a healthy attitude despite stresses and uncertainty in your life. A big indicator

here is the degree to which you are able to
maintain a grateful heart. The positive power of
a grateful heart is reliably miraculous.

- You are generally able to maintain a mentality
  of "love with detachment"—the gold standard
  for keeping your head on straight. It is a good
  idea to write down "Love With Detachment"
  somewhere and repeat it to yourself in challenging moments.

- You maintain a regular schedule that reflects
  your personal priorities. You do not drop out of
  a normal routine to constantly problem-solve or
  simply stand by to participate in unpredictable
  cycles of dysfunction. You consistently engage
  in activities you like.

- Your support relationships are active and
  meaningful to you. You avoid isolating.

- You have some sort of creative outlet. Journaling was (and is) very helpful for me. Others
  turn to music or creative projects, which can be
  surprisingly medicinal.

- You exercise regularly. No performance or
  intensity focus necessary here. Long walks (yes,
  even in foul weather) are powerfully positive
  for body, mind and soul. We have an unwritten

but iron-clad rule around my house. If someone asks "Wanna go for a walk?" the only acceptable response is "Sure!" I guarantee you will return feeling better than when you left.

- You are not over-indulging yourself. Obviously, drinking too much is not helpful in dealing with the burden of another's alcoholism. Overindulgence can also involve overeating and all sorts of other excesses. Be self-aware and stay in a healthy zone.
- You are leaning into some sort of higher-power relationship. Prayer, and finding peace in relationship with whatever higher power understanding you may have, is healthy and helpful.

Self-care and healthy coping is an ongoing process involving learning and intentionality. No matter how well you are doing, improvement is possible. Find what works for you and go there consistently. Steady as she goes, giving yourself a break along the way.

REGARDING ENABLEMENT

Enablement is a huge issue. It means protecting another from the consequences of their own behavior.

With enablement, the only thing harder than doing the right thing is knowing what the right thing to do is. Helping someone you love is understandable and noble, but enablement as a pattern with an addict can make the enabler complicit in disease progression.

Sometimes, a loved one is not aware of enablement until after the fact. I can recall giving cash in a birthday card, only to later

PROTECTING ANOTHER FROM THE CONSEQUENCES OF THEIR OWN BEHAVIOR.

ENABLEMENT AS A PATTERN
WITH AN ADDICT CAN MAKE THE
ENABLER COMPLICIT IN DISEASE
PROGRESSION.

SOMETIMES, A LOVED ONE IS NOT
AWARE OF ENABLEMENT UNTIL
AFTER THE FACT.

understand it was probably used to buy drugs. Don't
feel bad when you realize something well-intended you
did backfires as enabling. It is a learn-as-you-go sort of
thing. Improve your awareness, forethought and decision-making with experience.

The following are some typical examples of
enablement. I've done them all repeatedly. Can you see
yourself in any of these scenarios?

- Loaning money, even small amounts, with a
  promise you will be "paid back." In the case of
  an active substance abuser, cash is the closest
  thing there is to more of the substance of abuse.
  It will likely be used to buy more.
- Making excuses to others for miscues of the
  substance abuser. Making excuses helps the

substance abuser avoid accountability, which is
the opposite of what they need.

- Helping cover up or minimizing bad behavior
  of substance abusers. When loved ones find
  themselves telling white lies or skirting the
  truth, enablement is undeniable.
- Paying bills, tickets or fines for the substance
  abuser to help them avoid further expenses of
  late fees, etc. Think about this one. You pay the
  cost of someone else's poor choices? What sort
  of signal will this send when it comes to their
  future similar choices?
- Loaning your car to a substance abuser. Besides
  being risky, this once again helps the substance
  abuser avoid the consequences of the choices
  that rendered them without transportation.

These types of well-intended helping hands can
give cover for substance abuse to continue.

It is important to keep learning what does—and
more importantly, what does not—work as you go. Every
situation is different and loved ones are challenged to
learn what is helpful and what enables bad choices.

The addiction cycle will continue until some profound moment of truth crashes down. Enabling delays
this moment of potential reckoning and exposes the

addict to further deterioration, wreckage and possible demise.

Remarkably, the disease of addiction extends its power toward unhealthy behavior to loved ones. Like the addict, loved ones usually cannot see or control their own harmful behavior even though it is obvious to onlookers.

Enablement takes seemingly endless forms, with giving money to the substance abuser the most basic. With the exception of alcohol, other substances are typically a cash business. Abusers never seem to have enough cash, and early in the game, loved ones unwittingly fund the purchase of substances by giving or "loaning" the abuser cash. After a while, it becomes clear this is a bad idea but, unfortunately, the enablement continues in other ways. Loved ones do things like allow the abuser to use their car, move in for a while, pay bills or fines, replace lost or broken items such as cell phones and make excuses to others that protect the abuser. It is important to remember the definition of enablement, protecting another from the consequences of their own behavior, and make every effort to resist.

Oftentimes, wishful thinking is the pathway for enablement. For example, thoughts such as "He/she can stay with us for a while to prevent using. We can keep an eye on things and be here for support." Wrong. Substance abuse will continue right under your nose and there is nothing you can do to prevent it. You cannot prevent another person from destroying themself. In theory, you could search a substance abuser and their belongings for any contraband before allowing them back into your home or on your property, but that doesn't really work either.

YOU CANNOT PREVENT ANOTHER PERSON FROM DESTROYING THEMSELF.

Among the very best, most constructive things loved ones can do for a substance abuser is to learn about enablement and develop discipline to minimize it. Enablement is yet another face of the addiction monster for loved ones.

REGARDING TOUGH LOVE

"Zero tolerance" approaches withhold any sort of support if the substance abuser is not successful in recovery. It is the classic "love with detachment" taken to the fullest. Tough love can have a positive role in moving the substance abuser toward recovery as the consequences from substance abuse accumulate without relief being provided by others. The isolation and absence of a "safety net" can provide space for a natural, life-changing "bottoming out" experience to take place—which is a good thing, even if horrible to witness.

While there is value in not enabling, withholding any support whatsoever can be taken too far. Sometimes it is possible (and wiser) to "raise the bottom," which is not part of the tough love approach. This is particularly important when the bottom is death. Zero tolerance taken too far can result in refusing to help when doing so could have saved a life. This scenario could be a loved one's worst regret.

Another negative tradeoff with the tough love approach is the likely breakdown in relationship or communication between the substance abuser and loved ones. Despite the dysfunction, the relationship abusers have with loved ones may be a lifeline to eventual success in recovery. It is difficult to be a positive force when the relationship is on ice and you are out of communication. In fact, keeping lines of communication open no matter what is a valid strategy when committed to helping someone trapped in the hell of addiction. You never know when the chance to affirm or help facilitate treatment will arise.

A real danger with hardcore tough love is suicide. An addict can feel like the most important people in their life have abandoned them and there is no hope. In theory, these life-or-death eclipses can result in the addict hitting bottom, deflecting in a better direction. However, death as a bottom serves no one.

Tough love may be more appropriate with an SUD individual who does not have the disease of addiction because they likely have marginally more cognitive control. The brain malfunction associated with the disease of addiction renders the individual powerless over the substance. The abuser with out-of-control coping or self-medication behavior may still have a chance to make better choices.

The other side of the tough love coin is rescue. It is always a judgment call about attempting rescues. They generally don't work and make you appear to the user as a safety net again. In the case of our son Clay, the combination of his diabetes and Addison's disease was always life-threatening, even before throwing addiction into the disease mix. As a result, our rescue impulse was very strong during his adolescence and young adulthood.

We did execute a variety of life-saving drills. One involved my daughter flying to Los Angeles to hit the ground in search of Clay. The plan was to go to his last known location prior to going dark and start walking the streets looking. I had just made a similar unsuccessful attempt, only to learn Skid Row is really a place in Los Angeles. The squalor of filthy, broken bodies with hollowed-out eyes lying curbside was absolutely horrifying. Many of the figures lay in makeshift cardboard lean-tos, making it hard to know if they are dead or alive.

Our daughter's attempt this time led to finding her brother on a curb in desperate shape with both feet broken. She gave him water, power bars and first aid as if he was wounded on a battlefield. The desperately needed triage restored him enough to chase more meth even though unable to walk. I'll spare you the details and simply say the night ended with his first 5150 (involuntary 72-hour hold), taken away by ambulance under police supervision while strapped to a board.

Tough love has merits and is aligned with the notion of minimizing enablement. Taken too far, though, it can be tragic. I'm not a big fan of tough love because it can lead to a breakdown in communication and be a precursor to avoidable death.

REGARDING HITTING BOTTOM

The dance toward demise can be interrupted by "hitting bottom," experiences such as hospitalization, incarceration, acute despair or submitting to inpatient treatment. Hitting bottom always produces a wreckage field. Broken relationships, damaged health, lost jobs, self-loathing and financial reversal are par for the course. As bad as it is and as much is lost, hope survives. This dark, painful bottom too shall pass.

Hitting bottom can be a bounce to a better place—a new lifestyle of success in recovery. It is possible to move through the wreckage field to higher ground, now with the experience, humility and resolve needed for a better life. As absurd as it may sound, the bottom can be your friend. The memory of it can be your escort to a brighter tomorrow.

Unfortunately, bottoming out is not necessarily a once-and-done experience. Repetitive bottoms are all too common. A period of resolve and success in recovery can be followed by another cycle of substance abuse and despair. Sometimes, something absolutely terrible happens, and you're sure it will be a hitting-bottom experience—but it turns out not to be.

I recall one incident that involved my son driving into (through, actually) a building, hitting multiple other cars and then continuing to drive away—only to be arrested and jailed in the bowels of Los Angeles. All without access to his diabetes and Addison's disease medications. Gotta be a bottom, right? Wrong. After 48 hours in the clink, it was back on the street seeking more meth. In order to be a turning point, hitting bottom has to be real for the abuser, not the loved ones.

Of course, experiences like these are super frustrating for loved ones. Try not to despair if you have your own painful experiences around hitting bottom. Some sort of hitting-bottom experience seems necessary for most substance abusers to embrace treatment. Maybe like a baseball player, every at-bat is an important opportunity that eventually leads to getting on base—or into treatment.

REGARDING THE
TREATMENT MAZE

The treatment ladder goes like this: Detox → Residential Inpatient → Intensive Outpatient (IOP) with
Sober Living → Outpatient with Sober Living. Detox
and in-patient treatment include room and board in a
structured living environment.

It is important for loved ones to know that "signing
someone up for treatment" is not an option. The individual seeking treatment
must speak for themselves.
No treatment center wants
people who do not want to
be there. The law does not

"SIGNING SOMEONE
UP FOR TREATMENT"
IS NOT AN OPTION.

permit preventing someone from leaving. This might seem obvious as you read, but it can easily be forgotten in the heat of battle when you beg treatment centers, saying "Can't you please take him/her?" Most every loved one of an addict has wanted to, or tried to, "get them in treatment." It is okay to help identify options, check for open beds, research costs and insurance coverage possibilities. However, at the moment of truth, the afflicted person needs to speak up and ask for help.

"Interventions" have emerged as a possible way to pressure a substance abuser into treatment. Perhaps you have seen reality-show-type dramas featuring loved ones executing a coordinated plan to convince a user to capitulate and accept immediate transport to treatment. I know of cases where family members hired a professional "interventionist" to attempt personally engaging the substance abuser and escorting them to treatment. While these sorts of heroic efforts are understandable and admirable, chances of long-term success are probably very low. Capitulation leading to lasting change really needs to be intrinsic, reflecting personal choice and not a response to being pressured or overpowered.

If/when capitulation comes, it is always a good idea to immediately drive the person agreeing to treatment to check in ASAP. This is very important because the substance abuser's sick brain is constantly trying to rationalize why treatment is not really necessary. The "tomorrow" or "I can handle it" excuse can take over real fast, resulting in the individual changing their mind and refusing to cooperate, communicate or follow through.

Ideally, communication is already taking place with a treatment center and you know bed availability. The center will want to talk with the person receiving treatment and make sure they express commitment to treatment while screening for disqualifying conditions such as violent or suicidal tendencies, etc. There will be forms to fill out and payment negotiations to be resolved. Life is easier when you are organized. Invariably, the user is not organized and it can be helpful to have basic information at hand. A thorough search of an individual's person and possessions is required before clearing intake. Any contraband or items on the "not allowed list" will be confiscated with legitimate items securely stored until discharge.

TREATMENT "INTAKE" IS A HIGH-ANXIETY INTERVAL FOR EVERYONE.

Treatment "intake" is a high-anxiety interval for everyone. The patient's mind races with images of escape. They experience waves of fear about living without substance, losing freedom and being stuck in a place they don't like with people they don't want to be around. "Bouncing" out of intake to return to the street is brutal to see.

I recall pursuing my son like a rabid animal through the underbelly of Los Angeles, eventually coaxing him into conversation with his saintly therapist and me. After an intense interaction he, thank God, capitulated and agreed to enter detox/treatment. Traffic was bad and it took some time to get to the detox place. Clay started to fall apart on the way. He began the intake process and then his tortured mind changed. He declared he needed to get things in order first and would return tomorrow for sure. After dancing around the parking lot, with counselors in pursuit, he ran back into the streets of LA—sick, dirty, out of his mind and penniless. I didn't expect to see him alive again. The pain and sorrow was all I could bear. Over time, I came to understand the moment as just another stitch in time in the chaotic, broken world of addiction.

"Medical clearance" is also required to enter treatment. Treatment centers do not have full-time onsite doctors and are not equipped to provide meaningful medical care. This was frequently a complicating factor for Clay and our family. He always had to have his "kit," which included needles, vials and pills. As you can imagine, this type of thing was not welcome in environments full of drug addicts.

Drug tests become part of the routine in treatment and afterward in sober living. It is often expressed as getting a "UA" or being "UAed." While UA stands for urine analysis, there are a variety of drug test techniques besides urine analysis which has limited "last use" time capabilities. Many substances are not detectable in urine as soon as 48 hours after use. THC stays in your system longer—especially for heavier users, with heavier relating to both body weight and intensity of use. Hair samples can see back much further in time but cost more. I've noticed that sometimes individuals fresh out of recovery get buzz cuts and I wonder if it isn't symbolic of a clean start.

Substance abusers become experts on drug tests, oftentimes attempting to defeat them. They talk about it a lot and the cat-and-mouse game has become very sophisticated. Properly conducted UAs are witnessed and include verification screens such as sample temperature and checks for dilution. Drug tests are a very important and valuable deterrent to the user. Knowing they are subject to testing can be a powerful reason to stay clean. Home tests are available and vary widely in cost and accuracy. Having them on hand can be a good idea.

It takes some time to get a good feel for the treatment industry. Most people in the recovery or treatment business are in recovery themselves. Treatment programs provide employment for those succeeding in recovery and daily reinforcement to stay clean. It can be difficult for individuals with the checkered past common to substance abuse to find a job. Being able to work in the treatment field can be a real blessing and an important pathway to a better job and successful life. In addition, employees who are people in recovery themselves are more relatable and authentic in the eyes of someone considering recovery. Having a "been there, done that," "feel your pain" and knowing-the-ropes profile is a big plus for everyone involved.

It is worth taking a moment to survey the business landscape of the treatment industry. "Industry" implies some sort of organized infrastructure and is really not the right word. The "treatment industry" consists of innumerable small operations which are typically owned, operated and staffed by people currently successful in their own recovery. Think more along the lines of an ever-changing, loose network with lots of chaos. There are not really consistent standards program to program, especially in the case of sober living.

Some residential inpatient treatment programs have matured to include professional management, administration, processes and even marketing. They may cost more and assume clients have "good insurance" that they know how to bill for maximum payment. Hazelden Betty Ford is an example of a sophisticated nationwide treatment network.

Back to the treatment maze. Detox is the first step. It isn't always required if a person is not chemically dependent. If they are, a secure, medically supervised period is necessary for the body to stabilize without the substance(s) of abuse. This is a "blackout" period when no contact with the outside world is permitted. Loved ones should rest and rejoice in the relative safety of "being in" instead of bemoaning no updates or interaction.

Inpatient (residential) is the next step. A bed is assigned, roomate(s) are met, schedule and ground rules are provided and the journey begins. Group lectures, learning exercises, less frequent individual therapy sessions, meals and lights out make up the routine. Group therapy involves individuals sharing their stories and responding to prompts from the group leader. Inpatient treatment can last anywhere from 30 days to nine months. Longer is better. Trying to progress too far, too fast with steps that are too big is a common mistake. Our family made it. Repeatedly.

Our son was in inpatient treatment over 20 times, once for nine months, with every cycle involving the agony leading up to his capitulation and the decision to accept treatment. While much of the cost to our family was intangible—things like lost sleep and gray hair—the financial cost was high and seemingly never-ending.

Intensive outpatient (IOP) comes after inpatient. IOP requires nearly all-day sessions but does not include housing. The daily "group" format combined with weekly one-on-one counseling sessions continues as with inpatient. It can take some hustle to get IOP lined up. Unfortunately, it can also be easy to get kicked out. Attendance and participation are required to stay in IOP programs. Insurance won't pay if you don't go. The program doesn't want you without confirmation of payment, which is typically reconfirmed week by week.

IOP isn't always a step you only take after inpatient treatment. Lots of people are in circumstances where taking a month off would result in job loss, loss of income, etc., or going to rehab would be used against them in divorce/child custody proceedings, etc. There are people who go directly to IOP after they make a decision to attempt recovery. IOP is typically four hours a night for four nights a week in conjunction with AA meetings.

Attendance at Alcoholics Anonymous (AA)-type meetings is required during all phases of treatment. Sobriety groups are readily available in almost any geography.

Sober living housing needs to be found when the individual is coming out of a residential program that includes housing. In addition, insurance coverage for IOP often requires sober living. The sober living business has experienced widespread dubious (think illegal) arrangements between IOP Centers and sober living houses as they work together to maximize insurance reimbursements. Typically, individuals and loved ones are preoccupied with finding a place to live and don't care much about the business behind the scenes.

"Sober living" housing is an absolute free-for-all. Many "houses" are owned by recovering addicts who rent out beds, typically two to six in a room. They are commonly packed with chain-smoking addicts trying to stay clean. Dirty, loud and crowded is typical, as well as busy with people coming and going. Theft is a constant problem and privacy is not an option. House "rules," chore lists and curfews are taped to walls and refrigerators. Rules are variously enforced and the "house manager," who lives in the house, becomes an important variable in your life. Sometimes it is great with the house manager and sometimes it is not. Don't worry about it either way because houses and house managers come and go quickly.

When the owner, or house manager, decides to kick someone out for breaking the rules, it is typically swift. My son was "thrown out," sometimes into the dark, for eating other people's food, which was a chronic problem. In addition to being diabetic, he didn't have the discipline to buy food in advance. When diabetic "lows" inevitably hit, survival instincts kicked in and he would cram food into his mouth regardless of where it came from.

Failed UA drug tests are another way to get thrown out. Crazy as it sounds, Clay also had a urethra injury from falling as a kid and was sometimes unable to release urine. There is a maximum two-hour waiting period allowed before you are deemed to have failed the UA for failure to provide a sample. Failing the test (even if you didn't actually) requires expulsion from the house.

Most sober houses are detached single-family homes owned and operated by people experiencing success in their own recovery. They make a living from it because these operations are for profit. The sober house "market" can be bewildering. The quality of house environments runs the gambit from very good to absolutely horrific. Researching sober living options is something loved ones can help with; visiting the house and interacting with the house manager before agreeing to move in is highly recommended. It can work to "get in" somewhere for the benefits of the structured living and accountability of random drug testing and then continue to search for a better place.

We talked earlier about insurance and the help it is when finding and paying for treatment. Scholarships are sometimes available for people evidencing commitment to success in recovery without the ability to pay. They are often provided by people and organizations who understand the life-saving importance of treatment and want to help make it possible. It is always a good idea to inquire about the possibility of scholarship assistance.

REGARDING 12 STEP PROGRAMS

12-Step programs address the reality success in recovery is earned day by day. Ongoing resolve and support are necessary to *adopt* and *maintain* a successful recovery *mentality* and *lifestyle*.

The 12-Step framework to addiction recovery was pioneered by Alcoholics Anonymous (AA) to help people overcome alcohol abuse. The steps are considered spiritual principles designed to help an individual throughout their recovery journey. 12-Step programs have since been customized by various groups as a foundation for helping individuals recover from a wide range of addictions and harmful behavior patterns. Narcotics Anonymous (NA) is well established and a Godsend to many.

Advantages of 12-Step programs include being no cost/low cost and readily available. Being active in a community with others navigating recovery is a huge positive force for many.

12-Steps are a guide for a new way of living and thinking. They have provided a foundation for recovery for countless individuals. While no approach to recovery works for everyone, 12-Step programs are providing structure for life saving success in recovery.

KEY COMPONENTS OF 12-STEP PROGRAMS INCLUDE:

1. Overcoming denial. Being honesty about ones inability to control the destructive behavior of substance abuse
2. Capitulation. Surrendering to the existence of a higher power.
3. Embracing your higher power. Seek the will of God.
4. Self reflection. Bring into focus how one's behavior affects them self and others
5. Admission of wrongs in front of others.
6. Accepting and releasing the broken parts of oneself.

7. Having a humble heart. Understand we can not fix ourselves and turn to higher power for help

8. Acknowledging pain and harm caused to others by identifying in detail who was hurt and how we hurt them

9. Seek forgiveness.

10. Staying on track. Maintain success in recovery. Walk the talk. Do the work.

11. Spiritual development. Seeking will of higher power through prayer, meditation, self reflection and fellowship.

12. Service to others as an important element of how one lives

AA has its own "Big Book," which is sort of a Bible for those on a recovery journey. It is full of true stories about the experiences of others wrestling with SUD. These stories can be inspirational and educational. I found reading them to be emotionally intense at times. They were simple, true, plainly told accounts written by real-life people, each with a different lesson to learn.

"Meetings" are a foundational element of AA and success in recovery in general. They are held in all types of settings such as churches, community centers, non-profit facilities, treatment centers, etc., and take place all around the world. You could pause now, do a search for AA meeting times and find something close by. Specific AA meetings tend to take place at the same time and location on a weekly (or more) basis and have an established format and regular attendees.

Despite the goal of fellowship, meetings may not necessarily feel welcoming to newcomers. Part of it is just being a new person in an unfamiliar setting -which will wear off if you keep going. Meetings understandably can be controlled by the "Oldtimers"—similar to soldiers in Vietnam. Veterans sometimes hold off getting close to the new draftees because they would probably be dead soon, so why bother? Oldtimers fear that "newbies" will fall off the wagon so they wait until those folks have some significant sober time before they interact. All the more reason to keep going.

There are usually several AA groups to choose from (especially in a big city). It is a good idea to pick a group with members who share your socioeconomic status, background, etc. Find a group with which you are comfortable and make regular attendance a way of life.

There are also several types of meetings, with the traditional meeting including a mandatory opening statement by everyone who talks ("I'm John, I'm an alcoholic") followed by whatever they wish to discuss regarding their addiction. You will be shut down if instead, you drift into non-alcohol-related matters such as your drug abuse, divorce, etc. There are other groups for that, such as Narcotics Anonymous (NA), which are similar in format and support people in recovery from drug abuse.

There are also "Big Book study group meetings," Twelve Steps focus meetings and groups focused on specific demographics. Speaker meetings feature a long-time sober individual sharing his or her personal journey, which can be inspirational and encouraging. Keep with the basic meeting but expand into the others, as they can help maintain sobriety.

The notion of having a "sponsor" is a very import-ant AA tool. It is smart to ask someone to sponsor you. Listen to what potential sponsors share in meetings and find someone you respect based on what they have been saying and what you have in common with them.

Having and becoming a sponsor implies certain rules such as length of clean time and Twelve Steps progress. AA s twelfth and final step involves serving others, which includes being a sponsor. The role of a sponsor is to work with their mentee to make progress on the Twelve Steps, offer recovery guidance and be a call of last resort before relapse (which rarely seems to work). Finding and keeping a sponsor can be very hit-or-miss. No sponsor will interact with loved ones so don t even try to reach out. Doing so is not cool.

AA-type meetings are a microcosm of both life s burdens and blessings. Shattered lives mill around together, each broken in their own ugly way. The smell of pain cuts through cigarette smoke and body odor. Failures are palpable and everywhere, all while the blessing of hope flickers in the eyes of those making positive progress in recovery. In an oddly perfect way, the suffering encourages the wobbly to stay clean, while the positive spark of those reporting success inspires hope in others. Meetings are important for a reason.

REGARDING SUPPORT TEAMS

As with love, success in recovery is not possible alone. People around the user are important. They can provide needed structure, accountability and encouragement.

I fumbled to get an answer to a basic question faced by support team members. Is it okay to drink in front of someone in recovery? On the one hand, it seems like a basic courtesy and the least a person can do to be supportive, right? But what about the truth that this is real life and the person in recovery is going to be around people who may drink on occasion? If they can't stay on track around supportive people drinking responsibly, how can they stay on the wagon in the larger public?

What if the happy hour glass of wine is something you enjoy responsibly and find it disappointing to forego?

93

YOU WANT THE BIGGEST SUPPORT TEAM POSSIBLE.

What if the person in recovery says "Don't worry about it, doesn't bother me at all. I'd feel worse if you abstained just for me"? In the case of my family, it was hit-or-miss around our addict son. We were discreet and never drank in excess, but in hindsight, I probably should have abstained. (After writing this far, I was informed by a trusted friend personally challenged with alcoholism that drinking in front of an individual in recovery is a bad idea.) The individual already feels left out and different. It is much better to be considerate and substance-free in their presence.

You want the biggest support team possible, and service providers from treatment programs, medical professionals, law enforcement, sober house managers, etc. can be invaluable. The existence of a support team around a substance abuser can have a big impact on how "the system" responds to them. Substance abusers can be perceived as a lost cause by service providers if they appear to be alone in the fight or connected primarily to other substance abusers. In this case, they can be kicked to the curb, so to speak. The "system" can be an inhumanely cold machine. Most service providers are not willing to engage with a lost cause individual. However, if a struggling substance abuser has a visible support team expressing willingness to help support recovery, individual service providers will sometimes join the team.

Recruit team members by being authentic and communicating well. It is not unusual for a service provider to avoid sharing their personal contact information because if they did so regularly, they would be overwhelmed with communication and around-the-clock pleas for help. Nonetheless, it is possible to connect more personally with some providers if they are willing and able to provide more help. In these cases, get good at capturing names and cell numbers in real-time ("Can I pop you a text now in case it would be helpful to have my number?" etc.) Rejoice when a new person gives of themselves to help, and do not fret when they drop out or fade away, which is eventually unavoidable.

When interacting with service providers, be brief, clear and respectful of their time and mindshare. Texting is very efficient and much more likely to result in extended engagement than phone calls.

There can be lots of complexity and frustration around communicating with service providers. This varies depending on your geographical location and corresponding laws. In the U.S., for example, these complexities and frustrations around communication are due to our HIPAA laws. These laws require the individual receiving care to sign a release form permitting sharing of information. For risk management reasons, providers default to assuming a release is not in place and will communicate only when an active release is confirmed. This can get confusing because it is not uncommon for the person receiving treatment to change their mind and revoke release in the ongoing drama of their struggle. A powerful technique involves knowing that even if a provider is not authorized to share information, they can receive information from others. Reaching out to a provider to pass along information that would be helpful to them can result in them sharing info in return as a natural part of interacting. Sending FYI texts not requesting a response can be helpful and establish a stronger thread of connection. Project calmness and the desire to do good, and add value with every path you cross.

Interacting with the substance abuser provides an opportunity to show the love and support (not enablement) they surely need. Don't expect much love back. That is just how it goes. Addiction is a selfish thing.

Some of the best practices for a support team include:

- Know each other
- Capture contacts (except with AA sponsor)
- Communication
- Game planning

The support team should understand substance abuse "triggers" for the individual they are trying to support. Triggers are important and represent an area to make a positive contribution toward success in recovery; they are discussed in more detail in the following chapter.

REGARDING RELAPSE

"Relapse is part of recovery" is the well-worn handhold of hope for those suffering the pain and disappointment of relapse. It is a legitimate notion and hope should always be preserved. In cases of relapse, every effort should be made to "get back on the wagon" of sobriety as soon as possible. It is possible to experience an isolated "slip up" and immediately return to success in recovery.

Once stabilized and substance-free, the individual is faced with the

> RELAPSE IS PART OF RECOVERY" IS THE WELL-WORN HANDHOLD OF HOPE FOR THOSE SUFFERING THE PAIN AND DISAPPOINTMENT OF RELAPSE.

enormous challenge of maintaining "success in recovery." Unfortunately, the disease of addiction does not relent when an afflicted individual is sober. Quite the contrary, it intensifies. The diseased brain never stops substance-seeking, constantly rationalizing why "just one time" is okay. It's insidious, broken rationalization, like water pressing on a dam. It is a force that will not go away. One transient moment of lapse and the cycle starts again, typically escalating in intensity and danger over previous cycles.

The notion of triggers is very important in the ongoing struggle to avoid relapse. Triggers vary greatly by individual and require honest exploration to reveal. For example, being in a crowded, active environment may provide a safety zone for one person but invoke anxiety sufficient to be a relapse catalyst for another. Identifying and avoiding relapse triggers is a very important foundational step in recovery. Once an individual's triggers are identified, lifestyle should be tailored to avoid or minimize them. Loved ones and support team members should be aware of these triggers and support the individual in avoiding and coping with them (more on this later).

While relapse triggers vary by individual, there are some common, obvious ones. Some nearly universal triggers include: being around people the individual previously used with or people who are consuming substances; boredom; being alone or isolated; or significant life setbacks such as job loss, romantic conflict or relationship loss. The latter is an especially powerful relapse trigger. Feelings of "poor me" and "What does it matter?" are dangerous for the individual in recovery. Everyone should be on high alert when setbacks are experienced in the life of a substance abuser.

Curiously, success can be a powerful relapse trigger—a work promotion or raise, hitting clean time milestones or most anything representing accomplishment. Success is jet fuel for rationalization. The devil of rationalization never rests for the substance abuser. Thoughts like "If anyone deserves a drink, it's me" and "I can obviously handle it, look how good I'm doing" are examples of broken thinking looking for a chance to break through.

Ideally, there will be a plan to deal with unavoidable triggers when they are inevitably encountered—for example, alerting a loved one who can engage or be present to help get past the risky period. Anything

> THE DEVIL OF RATIONALIZATION NEVER RESTS FOR THE SUBSTANCE ABUSER.

that redirects the individual's focus to something healthy is helpful. Playing a musical instrument or leaning into whatever creative outlet the individual has can be very effective.

If you are struggling with an SUD, think in terms of a "slippery slope." Do whatever it takes to stay away from the edge. Let people help you by being accountable for not getting foolishly close to your slippery slopes.

Unfortunately, relapse can also be part of the "spin cycle" of addiction. The user enjoys the benefits of getting cleaned up in treatment all while subconsciously anticipating returning to using, over and over.

REGARDING EMERGENCY RESPONSE AND THE MEDICAL SYSTEM

Substance abuse is hard on the body, and if it persists, medical consequences will arise—sometimes slowly, hiding in the shadow of denial. Other times, it will come suddenly in the form of an accident or a serious medical event.

Emergency services (9-1-1) and the network of providers in the response chain are on the front lines of crises day in, day out. It is difficult, thankless work. They (and the system) did a very good job serving my son and family. They saved his life on a number of occasions. The contrast between different geographic locations was enormous. In the more rural environments, support was timely, friendly and compassionate. In the bowels of Los Angeles, things were different. Much different. The scale, intensity and relentlessness of human need quickly callous even the most compassionate first responders.

HAVING MEDICAL INSURANCE IS HUGELY IMPORTANT AND GREATLY AFFECTS THE CARE RECEIVED.

It is helpful to think of both the medical system and treatment maze in terms of levels of care. Having medical insurance is hugely important and greatly affects the care received. Emergency care is available to everyone but my experience is that having insurance greatly improves the quality, quantity and timeliness of care received. One of the most important things a loved one can do is ensure the person you are caring for has medical insurance. This is a really big deal. Low-cost/no-cost insurance is available through each state if the individual does not have insurance through work or other sources or is unable to afford private pay coverage. Do the research and do the paperwork. It is not that hard and can be life-saving.

For serious medical care, the point of entry is the hospital emergency room (ER). Getting there is always a traumatic process. Arrival can be via ambulance, loved ones, self-admit or occasionally law enforcement. It is not unusual for the suffering person to be uncooperative and erratic in behavior to the point things get physical. Emergency rooms can be chaotic and impersonal. The first step is check-in, which can feel like a barrier when you are desperate for medical attention. Pretty much the first question is "Do you have insurance?"

Emergency rooms are intended to support very short-term stays. The medical team wants to assess, stabilize and cycle out each patient as quickly as possible. Based on a physician's determination, patients can be released on their own or to a loved one, admitted to the hospital or sent to another location. In some cases, the patient requires hospital admission but no beds are available. This can result in being "boarded" in the emergency room until a bed becomes open. The "boarding" circumstance is terrible for both the patient and emergency room staff. The patient needs additional care and is stressed in the chaotic, loud emergency room setting. The medical staff needs the space and is not geared to care for stabilized but sick patients.

Hospital admission is the next level of care. Receiving ER services is not the same as being "admitted" to the hospital, which is referred to as "inpatient."

Hospital admission generally includes classifying a patient's medical condition like intensive care (ICU), critical, stable, etc.

Eventual hospital discharge is a very important step. By law, hospitals are required to confirm a "discharge plan" for any patient released. Patients can't simply be rolled down to the lobby and "released" if there is no reasonable plan for their safety and care. This step can briefly empower loved ones who may decline to take any responsibility for discharge plan duties if they believe the patient needs additional care and is not ready for discharge. The first couple of times through the process, loved ones can be anxious for discharge, believing they can help the patient bounce back in a more peaceful home environment. With experience, loved ones come to understand that left untreated, the underlying issue of substance abuse will reactivate the failure spiral, and so they resist discharge.

For example, the large metal pins surgically implanted in our son's feet eventually became infected. The raging staph infection was antibiotic-resistant, life-threatening and required a 24-hour-a-day intravenous drip of high-powered (expensive) antibiotics. The drip was required for 30 continuous days and the hospital wanted to discharge him, transferring care responsibility to loved ones supported by specialty nurses who offered training on daily IV maintenance and regular visitations. We declined as long as possible.

REGARDING LAW ENFORCEMENT

Is it just me, or has everyone had the fleeting thought of being a police officer? The role looks bigger than life. The truth is they are people just like the rest of us. My experience is that police are a "cut above" type of people. They generally do a difficult job honorably.

> POLICE OFFICERS HAVE SEEN IT ALL AND WILL WORK WITH YOU IF YOU WORK WITH THEM.

Police officers have seen it all and will work with you if you work with them. Have a collaborative attitude toward them; it will help them help you best. I personally have enormous respect and appreciation for law enforcement and make that clear right up front. Respect goes a long way toward recruiting new teammates in your effort to problem-solve.

Communication and cooperation are important. There is a school of thought that suggests you shouldn't tell law enforcement anything because it could be used against you or your loved one later. I suppose if criminality is a way of life that would be good advice, but I don't buy it for garden-variety encounters involving consequences of substance abuse.

I recall a time when Clay was pulled out of the desert by helicopter rescue after dark. He was lost with low blood sugar without his shoes and meds kit, about to face an unsurvivable desert night—until the authorities responded to his cell phone SOS signal to rescue him.

I followed Clay's distress signal as far as possible into the desert before being unable to continue, eventually tracking siren lights back to the main road. The cops were cool. I'm forever grateful.

It is not unusual for the substance abuser to engage in unlawful activity such as theft, possession of controlled substances or driving under the influence. If allowed to continue long enough, the individual is going to get in some sort of legal trouble. Odd as it may sound, it can be reasonable to hope the individual does get caught, considering the ordeal could be a catalyst for change or admission into treatment.

Law enforcement actually has several dimensions to it. In addition to officers on the street, there is the legal system, which is often activated by citations or charges issued against the substance abuser. In this case, a cloud of uncertainty forms over the substance abuser, and oftentimes also the loved ones who hope for a clean resolution. The system is very slow-moving and the cloud of prosecution or punishment can last indefinitely.

I'm familiar with a case involving a young man facing distribution of controlled substances charges at the felony level, which could lead to imprisonment. After not showing up a few times for hearings, the individual became a fugitive, which added significantly to his woes. The existence of arrest warrants prevented him from renewing his drivers license and accessing treatment/medical services, and it created an ever-present dread of being caught.

It is best to pay fines if at all possible before additional late penalties get added. It is also helpful to make progress in or toward recovery and share your commitment to recovery with a judge when the day finally comes to actually have a hearing. I'm not in a position to argue against having a lawyer if you can afford one, but telling your own story of regret, humility and commitment to recovery is powerful. The system is very biased toward leniency, especially for sincere individuals without long records who accept personal responsibility.

Restraining orders are another legal entanglement that sometimes come into play, particularly in cases of marriages or romantic relationships. Restraining orders typically prevent the accused individual from having any contact with the complainant, including coming within 500 feet of their residence. It makes sense to have a legal mechanism to protect innocent people from dangerous or unwanted interactions with one another.

Unfortunately, "restraining order abuse" is a real thing that can inflict terrible injustice. For example, when a woman makes false claims against a man—perhaps a husband or boyfriend who tries to leave due to her substance abuse or co-occurring condition—the courts have little choice other than to grant the restraining order in an abundance of caution for the woman's safety. This can result in a man being removed from his own home and children. Even though SUD affects both men and women, the adjudication process tends to be biased in favor of women and requires extended, expensive and painful appeals to eventually clear an innocent man. Even then, his reputation, finances and relationships, including with his own children, are significantly compromised.

The purpose of sharing this type of example is in keeping with the goal of this book: to provide helpful information. Obviously, both men and women are capable of all manner of egregious behavior, especially under the cloud and confusion of an SUD.

REGARDING MENTAL ILLNESS/
CO-OCCURRING CONDITIONS

"Co-occurring" is the term used to describe someone with both substance abuse and mental health disorders. The mental health condition can be organic (part of DNA) or activated by long-term substance abuse and/or environmental factors. If someone abuses substances heavily enough and long enough, they will end up in the co-occurring category. Acute depression can be brought on by substance abuse. This only stands

IF SOMEONE ABUSES SUBSTANCES HEAVILY ENOUGH AND LONG ENOUGH, THEY WILL END UP IN THE CO-OCCURRING CATEGORY.

to reason; prolonged use of mind-altering substances alters the mind and physical brain.

Life in the co-occurring world can be hell on earth for the afflicted individual and every person around them. Irrational, nonlinear periods of toxic intensity— or lifeless depression, unable to get out of bed—are hallmarks of mental illness. It can be bewildering.

There are a variety of mental illnesses. They can be hard to diagnose and even harder to treat. Acute depression, narcissism, bipolar and borderline personality disorder are a few. Borderline personality disorder is poorly named and arguably the most difficult to manage. Acute depression is just terrible and dark. The mania side of bipolar is dangerous and exhausting.

Mania is a dangerous and terrifying condition that involves abnormally elevated energy levels and hyperactive cognitive firing. Brain chemistry is overloaded with noradrenaline and spins out of control. The inability to sleep is a hallmark of mania. Sleeplessness can result from mania itself or be caused by abuse of certain substances such as methamphetamines or cocaine. The lack of sleep in combination with substance abuse can trigger out-of-control, wild-animal-like manic episodes. After several days without sleep, an individual will eventually begin to detach from reality and lose the ability to think and function rationally. Decision-making is severely compromised while impulsivity and flight of thought take over. The individual can lose the ability to care for themselves in the most basic manner such as eating, staying hydrated or keeping out of physically dangerous situations. God references or obsessions and grandiose thinking are common deeper into manic cycles. A psychotic break requiring medical and/or held-against-will intervention can be required.

Manic cycles build over time, sometimes weeks, and should be recognized and averted before growing deep roots and running their full course. Once again, the inability to sleep is an early sign of manic onset and the return of normalized sleep patterns comes late in the recovery process of manic cycles. There appears to be real physical brain damage associated with full-blown manic cycles, making it all the more important to recognize and treat mania early on.

A friend of mine unwittingly ended up in a marriage with a woman who suffered from both an SUD and what was eventually diagnosed as borderline personality disorder. The condition includes intense rage in response to rejection or its perception. My friend felt compelled to file for divorce, which of course added fuel to the fire in his marriage. She responded by filing false claims of physical abuse, which had my friend escorted out of his own home by the local sheriff and restricted from coming within 500 feet of his house as part of a rubber-stamped restraining order. One year later, he was eventually vindicated and allowed to go home. Upon arrival in freezing temperatures, he found the house severely trashed, windows and doors wide open with the heat turned up to 90. His most important personal property such as photo albums, file cabinet contents and laptops were in a bathtub full of water. On top of the pile was human defecation assumed to be that of his estranged wife.

Individuals afflicted with co-occurring conditions can engage in very shocking behavior. Even though there is no contest for craziest stores, there are countless people with competitive nightmares. If this is you, please hang in there. Like my friend, you can endure and live under sunnier conditions.

Discussion of mental illness in any detail is beyond the scope of this book, but as you can imagine, co-occurring cases are extremely challenging. To begin with, there are not nearly enough qualified psychiatrists, and they are the only ones who prescribe psych meds. Unlike medical specialties such as coronary care, we are not yet very good at mental health medicine. The science and best practices have yet to mature. We have much to learn, and even the best practitioners appear to fumble in the dark with patients who are difficult to diagnose and treat.

While not a mental illness per se, psychotic breaks are a real, acute occurrence of mental instability. A psychotic break involves a distinct break from reality; the individual becomes disconnected from the real world. Psychotic breaks can result from stress on the mind and body. For example, days without sleep due to substance abuse can lead to a break from reality. Manic episodes depriving an individual of sleep for extended periods can have the same effect. Been there, done that with our son. Not pretty, to say the least.

Policy Note Regarding Homelessness: Most chronically homeless have a co-occurring condition. This is why "housing first, no preconditions" solutions to homelessness are nonsense. These people need inpatient treatment, which by definition includes shelter. Housing without preconditions is institutionalized enablement. The government (think some sort of publicly-funded agency or program) becomes complicit in further damaging people by extending the time to hitting bottom and a change of lifestyle. Addicts will use until some external force stops them (recall our hitting bottom discussion).

On the mental health side, bad policy got us here in the first place. The United States had an extensive infrastructure of institutionalized mental health facilities and associated resources. The number of mentally ill who are unable to live independently in society is a function of population. A certain percent of any population falls into this category. We had a mental health infrastructure reasonably sized for the number of patients.

Then the entire system was pretty much torn down. Well, to be fair, the physical campuses were not torn down; they were abandoned. Many years later, some campuses were repurposed for uses like universities. California State University Channel Islands Campus is an example.

The "feel-good" policy at the time was suddenly "people should not be warehoused" and they should have an opportunity to "live in the community." Unfortunately, local capacity to serve the mentally ill was not put in place. Residents were released en masse, the population continued to grow and homelessness became visible. The policy error was egregious. We already had what was needed: safe, secure housing, structured living environments, medication management, efficient on-site health care, socialization and programming options, access to fitness and library facilities, etc. This taxpayer-funded system was unbelievably abandoned while putting the very people intended to benefit in harm's way.

REGARDING PSYCH MEDS

Psych meds can be necessary, and finding the right combination is an excruciating hit-or-miss exercise in slow motion. Meds are introduced in small dosages and "tapered up" over the weeks to see what happens. Sometimes there is improvement, lots of times there is not, and there are always side effects. If the Rx regimen is deemed to not be effective or is causing intolerable side effects, the meds are tapered down and different drugs are introduced. The process can go

PSYCH MEDS CAN BE NECESSARY, AND FINDING THE RIGHT COMBINATION IS AN EXCRUCIATING HIT-OR-MISS EXERCISE IN SLOW MOTION.

123

on indefinitely in search of a meds lineup that brings relief worth the side effects. All the while, the patient is either questionably compliant or doesn't even show up for appointments. Beware, patients also may not be accurate or truthful in reporting what they have been experiencing.

Psych meds come with all sorts of negative side effects. It is unnerving to read the warning disclaimers because the lists of potential side effects are long and scary. They often include things like weight gain, skin rashes, sleep disruption, energy loss, involuntary tics, etc. Many times, a patient needs to taper down and discontinue the use of a psych med because of intolerable side effects, even when it does seem to help psychologically.

Perhaps the most troubling side effect involves the cloud of suicide risk. Many psych meds can cause suicide ideation and actual suicide as potential risks. Obviously, suicide is a worst-case scenario. Your mind wretches the first time you are presented with the possibility. Unfortunately, it seems you can't unring the bell once this risk registers in your mind. The burden of knowing it is a possibility can become its own sidebar nightmare. To make matters even worse—if that is possible— impulsivity is also a common side effect of some psych meds. Clearly, suicide ideation and impulsivity are not a good combination.

It is not helpful to dwell on the idea of suicide as a risk, but it should be on your radar. My daughter lost a sorority housemate and close friend to suicide about fifteen years ago. The girl was pretty, popular, smart and musically gifted. No one ever imagined she would take her own life. Ultimately, the tragedy was tied to the side effects of a medication she was on. On one hand, I want to apologize for even introducing this topic, but it is part of the co-occurring challenge and you should be aware.

The entire circus dance around psych meds is further complicated by forces such as continued substance abuse and poor personal care routines. Sleep, nutrition, exercise, stress levels and healthy socialization all tend to be off the rails during this time. As a result, the individual "presents" to the psych doctor as needing more or different psych meds, which may make the search for stability and peace even more difficult.

Many times, if a patient is able to get back to relative normal, they quit taking meds, arguing they feel fine and don't need them. Can you guess what happens then?

Sadly, psych meds were the heavy hand in my son's passing. After nearly four years of success in recovery, Clay was able to manipulate an elderly psychiatrist to prescribe pretty much anything he wanted. Clay was very bright, knowledgeable and easy to like.

He was able to get monoamine oxidase inhibitors (MAOI)-class meds prescribed. These types of drugs are not appropriate for addicts but were the best available proxy for the meth effect Clay sought. Ritalin prescriptions set off a multi-year rolling relapse. Along the way, Clay was able to try the entire menu of meds that interested him (including Modafinil, used to stay awake) and ended up in an intense relationship with a medication called Nardil. Nardil provided benefits he really liked: increased confidence, drive, focus and energy. He denied Nardil's undesirable effects of sleeplessness, impulsivity, risk-taking, relapse and flight of thought, which in turn led to medical instability, psychotic breaks and hospitalization.

Unbelievably, hospitals and the medical system conspired in Clay's demise. You see, when admitted to a hospital, the protocol is for attending medical staff to continue a patient's "home" prescriptions, which in Clay's case included the devil of Nardil. So they kept giving it to him! I was able to intervene a couple of times and got Nardil temporarily withheld but always lost out to the system's rule of giving him Nardil even though it was obviously wrong. One doctor is very reluctant to override another doctor's Rx, especially when it involves a psych med.

REGARDING INVOLUNTARY
PSYCHIATRIC HOLD

Every state has laws governing "involuntary holds" of individuals deemed to be an imminent threat to themselves or others. The hold is called "5150" in California, reflecting the statute code governing involuntary holds. An order from a qualified medical professional and a special crisis team is typically required. The hold is not an arrest but rather an involuntary psych hold. If medically stable, the held person is usually brought to a county psych hospital, which are dreadful places. The held patient receives minimal treatment, usually involving sedatives aimed at stabilizing them enough to avert the immediate crisis. There is an adjudicated process to extend holds over 72 hours if deemed necessary.

If not medically stable, the individual will likely be brought to a traditional hospital until "medically cleared" for admission to a psych facility. My son had a complicated medical profile and cycled through this system repeatedly. The first time involved broken bones (crushed heels) in both feet, rendering him unable to stand, all while chemically dependent and injecting methamphetamines. He was raging for more meth, using it openly. As crazy as it sounds, meth was not the most pressing problem. His Addison's disease and diabetes put him in danger of coma and rapid death in the case of physical injury without prompt intramuscular injections of stress dose steroids.

In this particular case, my daughter was at the scene after making an emergency dash to LA in an effort to locate Clay. She, with the help of an army of angels, was able to get Clay to inject the steroids needed to forestall adrenal collapse (coma) due to Addison's disease, and secure a 5150 involuntary hold order from Clay's saintly recovery therapist, all while having him physically restrained long enough to be strapped to a board and carried away by the professionals.

REGARDING WHAT SUCCESS IN RECOVERY LOOKS LIKE

You can tell when someone is authentic in recovery. They express thoughts full of humility, gratitude, personal responsibility and reliance on their higher power. The importance of this type of mentality is well-known in the recovery community. Some individuals struggling to build positive momentum will express these sentiments but fail to be consistent or unable to live like they talk. Be kind. Give them a break and lean into the positive things they say even if words and actions don't yet line up. The notion of faking it until you make it has some merit.

Seeking pleasure or relief is in itself not a bad thing. We are human and all do it. The challenge is to do

> SUBSTITUTING CONSTRUCTIVE OUTLETS TO REPLACE DESTRUCTIVE SUD BEHAVIORS CAN BE A POWERFUL TOOL.

so in a constructive, healthy way. Substituting constructive outlets to replace destructive SUD behaviors can be a powerful tool. Creative outlets such as playing music or pursuing a hobby can offer a super helpful substitute that brings satisfaction. Physical activities or sports can also be very helpful as a substitute. Many recovery environments include weightlifting equipment, music rooms and/or gym memberships. The trick is to not deny pleasure-seeking but rather develop healthy ways to experience satisfaction. If you see someone in recovery who goes a bit overboard with a particular passion, that is generally healthy; consider it a good sign and add positive energy to their passion.

> THE TRICK IS TO NOT DENY PLEASURE-SEEKING BUT RATHER DEVELOP HEALTHY WAYS TO EXPERIENCE SATISFACTION.

Regularly attending AA-type meetings is a foundational part of success for many. They talk about the importance of "not forgetting" where they came from and remaining "plugged into" a recovery lifestyle.

The person achieving success in recovery tends to be straightforward in letting others know "I don't drink" when the moment calls for it. Any sort of detailed sharing is not necessary, but when offered a substance, they tend to say "I don't drink" rather than something like "Not now." It doesn't take long for people around the person in recovery to get the hint and avoid pushing alcohol (or anything else) on the person. The person in recovery becomes comfortable with the teetotaler element of their identity. Individuals at risk in recovery tend to avoid this label, leaving open their opportunity to consume without confusing or alarming others.

The following traits are external signs of success in recovery:

- Meeting attendance consistent (stopping is a bad sign)
- Dependable/reliable. Keeps a consistent schedule
- Sponsor relationship active. Could be either as a sponsor or a person being sponsored
- Talks about specific goals and aspirations
- Faith group connection active

- Journaling
- Financial position improving
- Smoking, vaping, caffeine use down or gone

Many individuals successful in recovery will credit a higher-power relationship for success so far and invoke it for continued success going forward. This spirit-centered way of living reflects humility, which lines up with the notion of being powerless over substances and many of life's circumstances. Recovering addicts have a lot to teach the rest of us about humility.

As I write this, I'm hard-pressed to think of anyone living successfully in recovery who is not transparently centered in their higher-power relationship. The Christian framework of Jesus Christ as the son of God who died and arose to forgive our sins is widely embraced in the recovery community. It is a messy but profoundly beautiful thing. While for some Jesus is their foundation of faith, it does not have to be. Embracing a force greater than yourself is the common denominator for success in recovery. Finding one's faith goes a long way toward increasing the odds of success in SUD recovery.

Key relationships begin to mend, even strengthen, for the person living successfully in recovery. Family ties can often be restored as communication and accountability improve. It is actually possible for ongoing success in recovery to provide a backdrop for richer relationships than would otherwise be possible, given the shared experience of working through adversity. Other relationships associated with substance abuse behavior will fall away.

Sometimes, a fresh start away from people associated with substance use and prior failures is required. Some of the most inspirational people living healthy lives of success in recovery talk of turning points that involved making a "clean break" from old contacts. Some relocated to start over. Transitions this drastic may not be possible but are examples of the importance of a hard lifestyle pivot.

REGARDING TRIGGERS

Triggers are important and real. These are conditions that endanger a person's ability to stay on the right track in the moment. Think about feelings you experience when hearing certain songs from your youth. While

TRIGGERS ARE IMPORTANT AND REAL.

the emotion washing over you from hearing a song is innocent, for the addict, triggers can bring emotions that activate a strong desire for their substance of choice. This could be the smell of an illicit substance or loud music previously associated with using. Being alone and bored is a huge trigger for many.

Evidence of a person's strength in recovery is knowing, avoiding and communicating their triggers. Their support teams know what specific triggers are and help to avoid them and/or take steps to mitigate risk when triggers are unavoidable. Such teamwork is impossible unless the person in recovery has previously communicated clearly and honestly.

An example of proactively dealing with triggers is not living alone, understanding doing so is a relapse risk. Other examples would include avoiding environments where substances are being used and not having contact with people who an individual used to consume substances with.

REGARDING THE
SLIPPERY SLOPE

This is probably the most difficult and important chapter in this book. Let's revisit some of the key ideas we have covered so far and connect the dots in a way that will be helpful, perhaps even life-saving for some.

As we explored previously, SUD occurs on a continuum with the disease of addiction on one end and temporary, moderate substance abuse on the other end. The individual with the disease of addiction absolutely must abstain from all mind-altering substances to avoid full-blown relapse and all the life-destroying issues it brings. The temporary, moderate substance abuser has the potential to mature and learn so that they may be able to drink moderately (for example) without falling down the slippery slope into the pit of abuse, despair and self-destruction.

So how do you know where someone is on the continuum? Can they live a life that includes safe contact with mind-altering substances (or activities such as gambling)? Recall the persistent, dark power of rationalization and denial in the mind of someone with an SUD. Does even acknowledging the possibility of anything other than 100 percent, lifelong abstinence foolishly undermine success in recovery? These difficult and important questions can only be answered on a case-by-case basis. Start by revisiting the diagnostic protocol for the disease of addiction in the Substance Use Disorder vs. Disease of Addiction chapter.

If the criteria or your lived experience suggests you are an addict, then accept it. Full stop. Don't overthink it. Don't let the fact others may not have the disease serve as rationalization you don't either. Complete, lifelong abstinence from all mind-altering substances is the only safe path forward for you. Do whatever it takes to adopt this mindset, and then never allow yourself to be drawn into re-deciding again later. The condition does not go away. Remember all the "clean for 20 years, then suddenly died of overdose" stories you have heard. Choose to live. Get and stay clean. Period.

If you are on the disease end of the SUD continuum, don't be taken in by the increasingly popular notion of "California clean" that suggests THC (marijuana) or mushroom ("non-addictive" hallucinogenic) consumption is acceptable in recovery. The argument is along the lines of "It helps me stay chill and not use other more dangerous substances" and "I can handle it, THC really helps me."

Have you ever heard an overweight, out-of-shape person speak with confidence about how to get fit? Or perhaps a financially-strapped person talking about how to make money? We all have. There is obviously a glaring credibility gap in these types of situations. In the case of someone living in the wreckage of mind-altering substance abuse, talking about how THC helps them seems more suitable for a comic strip than helpful advice for others striving for success in recovery.

KEEP THE SLIPPERY SLOPE IN MIND.
HOW CLOSE TO THE EDGE CAN YOU
GET WITHOUT SLIDING INTO THE
ABYSS? DO YOU REALLY WANT TO
KNOW, GIVEN THE ONLY WAY TO FIND
OUT IS TO SLIP BACK INTO THE PIT?
IF AN ALCOHOLIC HANGS AROUND

THE BAR TO PLAY POOL OR BE WITH
FRIENDS, HE/SHE WILL GO OVER THE
EDGE. IT IS ONLY A MATTER OF TIME.
WHY EVEN GO NEAR THE EDGE?

Are you familiar with Russian roulette? It is an outrageous game of risk that involves loading a single bullet into a revolver, spinning the chamber and betting on your survival as the trigger is pulled with the gun pointed to your head. Even though the odds of winning may be favorable, no right-minded person would play the game. The risk of relapse is like that when an addict goes near the slippery slope.

One of my casual hobbies is archery. When making life decisions, I sometimes think of the Robin Hood scene involving a bow and arrow used to shoot an apple off someone's head. If the shot is not perfect, would it be better off a little high or a bit low? If you are going to err in efforts to be successful in recovery, err on the side of caution. Like the archery example, doing so could be the difference between life and death.

It is wiser and better to err on the side of sobriety if substances are an issue. I have two dear friends of extraordinary accomplishment who have tragic SUD stories involving their parents and immediate family members. They both have committed to lives of total abstinence, reasoning that the risk of activating an SUD is just not worth any benefit from consuming. Besides, they want to live as their best selves and be good examples for others in their family who are susceptible. "California clean" might work for someone who experienced SUD as a temporary rough patch and has resolved underlying issues. The notion is risky business for the person with, or closer to, the disease of addiction.

REGARDING THE ODDS

Attempting to get a feel for the odds of permanent success in recovery can be a very unsatisfying effort. Unlike typical medical conditions with precise data on outcomes, SUD outcomes are essentially unknowable. I asked everyone and anyone, only to receive responses like "Every case is different," "You never know" and "I don't know the odds, but know they are not very good with the disease of addiction."

Prospects for success in recovery and a full, joyous life vary by situation and are directly related to where one falls on the SUD continuum. There are living examples of success from all across the continuum. Some of the most inspiring people I know have overcome extremely dark periods under the cloud of SUD and built on the experience to lead powerfully positive lives. Their challenges with SUD equipped them with resolve and faith that took them to higher levels of joy, influence and meaning. Reasons for hope are clear and present.

Obviously, chances of success are also directly related to knowledge and choices made by the affected individual, and to a lesser extent their support team.

It is reasonable to think technology and our understanding of the human brain will bring improved success pathways over time. There are alternative treatment approaches emerging that have the potential to be helpful for some. For example, I'm aware of an individual who had SUD challenges stemming from post traumatic stress disorder (PTSD) after serving in the Vietnam War. He found lasting relief with physician-supervised therapy, which included use of ketamine—a dissociative anesthetic with hallucinogenic effects. Apparently, therapy while under the effects of ketamine allowed release of underlying psychological burden and the desire to self-medicate with substance abuse. Others with different unresolved trauma profiles have reported similar success. I'm absolutely not suggesting this or any other alternative treatment; I am observing we have much to learn and the future may bring about new, potentially effective therapies. **KEEP HOPE ALIVE.** Keep hope alive.

Reading this book is proof of your desire to learn more and get better at taking the next right steps—perhaps not for yourself, but for someone you love. In some ways, reading *Regarding Substance Abuse and Addiction* will fall short because it does not provide all the answers. It doesn't provide definitive answers, either; there are none. Hopefully it does, however, add to your knowledge and insight in a way that contributes to your story in a meaningful and positive manner, whether you personally struggle with an SUD or are in relation with someone challenged by SUD.

Could it be that the way we act out our roles is as important as how the drama ends? There is great wisdom in remaining centered in love and doing your very best from moment to moment. The knowledge you did so will be a profound comfort all the days of your life.

May God bless you, my fellow traveler.

Note to friends and family: *If you are a personal friend or family member and learn of accounts mentioned in this book for the first time, you may wonder why you didn't know or why I didn't share these types of experiences sooner.*

What purpose would passing stories around have served? My son, Clay, already had a full plate of challenges. The last thing a dad wants to do is increase his burden by making it a topic of conversation for others. I did try to share sometimes, but it really was asking too much of the listener. Besides, they couldn't really help.

It is okay to talk about anything now if it can be helpful to another.

REGARDING WHAT
HAPPENED WITH CLAY

Remarkably, and after tremendous effort, Clay's fall was from the top. In some ways, it was a beautiful thing. Let me explain.

As we have explored together in this book, life for someone with the disease of addiction includes slipping into deep, dark places, followed by climbing up and out—often only to repeat. It is not uncommon for the lows to become progressively lower and the highs more hard-fought.

In Clay's case, his final climb was to levels of accomplishment even higher than we dared to imagine. He was ridiculously smart, which was evidenced by things like doing calculus to relax—which sounds impressive, but honestly, it was frustrating to watch so much potential being wasted in the addiction/recovery spin cycle.

In the early fall of 2022, Clay was struggling as usual and living in Los Angeles (not an easy place). He started applying for jobs as a data analyst. He had a biology degree from California State University and was able to cobble together a decent resume (if you overlooked all the gaps in employment and lack of career progress). He scored a phone interview with a highly respected Department of Defense contractor providing sophisticated, classified analytics service to the military. Clay told them he already had another job lined up (low-level work as an hourly contractor) but was interested. It was hard for companies to find capable technical talent at the time and the company quickly made Clay a terrific job offer without the normal interview process.

The job was in San Diego. Clay didn't want to leave LA and was living on the ragged edge of functionality. He accepted the job, which included pay, benefits and a professional package way over anything reasonably considered possible for him at the time. He had three weeks to report for work with the understanding he would need to obtain Secret-level security clearance with the federal government due to the nature of the data he would be working with.

It was not clear if Clay would be able to get it together in time to show up on the appointed Monday morning. The Friday before, he was still in LA with no plan for getting to San Diego. After some pretty intense suspense and conversations, he rolled into San Diego just before sunset on Sunday, looking for a sober house. After a couple of misses, he found a house that would take him. As is often the case, we were grateful for the positive opportunity and braced with dread for another disappointment. Would he make it on time in the morning? Would they be startled by his condition and turn him away?

He made it. Amazingly, the expansive offices were empty except for security personnel. Everyone was working remotely and things were done electronically or by teleconference. The HR and security processing began and Clay was free to come and go as he wished. Since he didn't have security clearance, they couldn't give him much to do other than company orientation and low-level data crunching-type stuff. The slow, soft start ended up being a God thing for good.

Clay settled into a routine of going to the office (to get coffee at first), accomplishing what little they had for him to do and getting off to a positive "Zoom inter-action" start with his East Coast-based supervisor and scattered teammates. It was the norm for him to be one of the only employees working in the building. With so much free time and a deluxe setup, Clay began working on obtaining data analytics credentials through online certification programs. He racked up a few and built his confidence and work ethic while casting himself in a positive light.

The Secret security application and clearance process was unbelievably rigorous and could take six to nine months to complete. The low pressure, low visibil-ity and high pay with full benefits interlude gave Clay an opportunity to reinvent himself. He got a reliable car, found a solid sober house, joined a church, started to save money, received written praise from superiors at work and started seeing a couple of girls—good girls who saw his heart and wanted him. While these things may sound routine to a healthy person, they represented an array of high-water marks for Clay. His years in and out of treatment did not permit the relationship and life foundation formation opportunities most of us take for granted. This is the beautiful part I mentioned, bonafide validation of what he was capable of: healthy connec-tions and acceptance he was never able to enjoy before.

He called daily to talk about goals, progress and generally positive things. He talked about accepting Jesus and his pursuit of a relationship with the Lord. He regularly told me he loved me and my wife. He grew even closer with his sister, who coincidentally lived in San Diego's hip Ocean Beach area. This period of progress was profoundly meaningful, particularly given all our years on the other side of the coin.

In the back of our minds, we knew the inappropriately obtained Nardil prescription Clay was beholden to (see the Psych Meds chapter) brought him "upside" benefits of energy and confidence, all while posing risks of mania and impulsivity; recall that Nardil is an MAOI-class drug not suitable for addicts. We had long ago accepted the fact it is not possible to control another person's choices and were taking each day one at a time, attempting to remain joyous in spirit along the way.

My wife's birthday is in May and I had been asking her how she wanted to celebrate. I was expecting a travel adventure would be in store, as she usually wanted to be away and out of sight for birthdays; some sort of subconscious avoidance of aging, I suppose. This time, she surprised us all by saying she wanted to spend a couple of nights with Clay and our daughter at the Paradise Lodge on Mt. Rainier. Despite living in the

Pacific Northwest for 30 years, she had never been to Mt. Rainier National Park. We pulled it off, extending the celebration to include my birthday, which is in early June.

Our time together was nothing short of heavenly—perfect sunny blue skies, snow still adorning world-class scenery, long hikes, good meals and Clay talking about his career and the two young ladies who both professed to love him. The moments shared were the apex of special time together for our little family. We parted with hugs, dropping the kids off at Seatac Airport. It was the last time we saw Clay alive.

Clay wore a continuous glucose monitor that transmitted blood sugar readings to his phone as a tool to help manage his diabetes. My phone would get alarms when sugar levels fell dangerously low. At about 4:30 AM on July 1, alarms started rolling in. My wife and I scrambled by calling his phone over and over and then eventually other people who knew Clay to ask for help. We eventually woke up his house manager in San Diego who said Clay went to LA for the weekend. Oh, that sinking sensation, when it feels like all your blood drains to your feet, your heartbeat jumps around and your chest feels heavy. We eventually exhausted every possible outreach and had to wait.

We live on the water on one of the San Juan Islands in Washington State. I took a solo beach walk that climbed through the woods before circling back. The beauty, especially around dawn and dusk, is nothing short of breathtaking. This time, my breath was being held shallow by a force unseen. I already knew what I didn't want to know. We had been to the door of demise countless times before, but this time, it felt different; it was still and empty, not the usual frenetic fight inside. Later that morning, we got the call from our sobbing daughter who was contacted by an LA hospital.

Clay was brought to the hospital around 3:00 AM in critical condition by a friend who didn't stick around. His body temperature was over 106 and all sorts of life-threatening medical conditions were colliding. He was pronounced dead at 6:40 AM and methamphetamine-type drugs were found in his system. Clay had told us and seemed to understand, given his profile and history, he would not survive ever using meth again.

The ground shook. We learned about the pain of loss. About grief. About *things that matter*. I began to write, including the following passages regarding grief:

Tears

Tears drip
Slowly
Lonely
One at a time
Then stop

Then one more

Grief

Grief is your friend
Purifying one's heart
Cleansing one's soul

Grief is sneaky
It swells up out of thin air
Rolls in unexpectedly
Uncontrollably
Sometimes with force and speed that physically
convulses

Paralyzing speech
Compressing respiration
Accelerating pulse
Often unleashing a torrent of tears.

Embrace it.
Resist not
Deny not
Hide not
Rush not

Let it wash over
The agony is real
But it won't last long

Successive waves eventually diminish in intensity.
And become oddly comforting.

Rejoice in the relief that follows
Knowing each wave brings healing
Adding layers of experience, maturity, wisdom
and richness.

Count grief as yet another of life's innumerable
blessings.

Seek comfort in the Lord.
It is there to be found.

The process of seeking answers, return of remains, etc. was awful and unlikely to be helpful to a reader. Given this book's goal of helping others, I'll skip this part with the obvious suggestion of not passing away alone in the bowels of LA.

I thought seriously about suing the malpracticing psychiatrist who enabled Clay's addiction along the way and then continued to recklessly prescribe Nardil, which we believe undermined his recovery. After a cursory review of the facts and evidence, it became clear we had a compelling case and would likely win a substantial monetary award. I'm not motivated by money, however, and imagined any proceeds would be used to support others dealing with SUD.

After ruminating, we chose to let it go. Why, you ask? Several reasons. To begin with, seeking legal recourse is a negative process we have little appetite for. Life is too short. Additionally, ensuring the accountability of others is not my job. Let's leave that to a higher authority. Also, to be honest, Clay knew what he was doing. Nothing we can do will bring him back. If this doctor wasn't his nemesis, another eventually would have been. Most importantly, there are more positive ways to move forward and support those impacted by

SUD, more fulfilling ways to do good in the world—like writing this book for you, perhaps.

A new chapter in the story of our family, and each of our individual lives, began. Yes, the initial pages of this new chapter were filled with pain and loss. The door slammed shut to untold possibilities and unfulfilled potential. To lose a child hurts like nothing else. For the child to be an only son...

But then more pages turn. And they are good. The glorious journey of the gift of life continues for those of us left behind. My little family moves forward with a wide base of positive understanding. We did everything humanly possible to support Clay; he knew it, and our bond of love and relationship never faltered, even under extreme pressure. Clay attained a level of accomplishment that validated his potential and was higher than we had the boldness to expect. Clay was affirmed and loved by others, which is an even bigger deal for all of us. Clay came to a faith relationship with the Lord, which gives us confidence in our eventual reunion.

My sister escorted our broken daughter from San Diego and spent sacred days grieving with us. It was beautiful. My wife and I have always enjoyed a wonderful relationship and the experience of losing a child only served to press us further together. The shared pain brought us to an intimacy beyond the reach of words. Dare we ask for more or better?

If that is not enough to be thankful for, I was released, so to speak, and am experiencing a positive personal renaissance with aspirations to be a blessing to others. The time, energy and capacity so long reserved to support Clay has been freed up. I've discovered writing and continue to cycle and kayak, living and loving at the level of a much younger man. Despite enjoying a rich, blessed life I have no doubt even better years lie ahead.

If you are interested in more insights about how the door of loss opened new understanding and vitality in my journey thus far, consider reading my first book, *Regarding Things That Matter.*

With love and encouragement,
CRAIG A WILLIAMSON

An accomplished athlete and natural leader, Craig's global adventures and professional achievements are matched by his deep commitment to family and nation. His personal experiences, including the tragic loss of his only son in 2023, deeply influence his perspectives and drive his mission to inspire and support others.

A resident of Washington State's San Juan Islands with a second home in Scottsdale, Arizona, Craig is an avid cyclist and wilderness enthusiast. Despite his achievements, he maintains a low profile, focusing on living a meaningful life and being a blessing to others.

www.ingramcontent.com/pod-product-compliance
Lightning Source LLC
LaVergne TN
LVHW091218080426
835509LV00009B/1055